IMAGES
of America

DEXTER

Around 1890 the boys of the Elkinstown Club on Lake Wassookeag were building a well house, and someone got the idea to stage a fake hanging. From left to right are: Bert Call, Charles Wyman, Harry Hale, Wint Fay, and Dr. Charles Ryan.

IMAGES
of America

DEXTER

Frank E. Spizuoco

ARCADIA
PUBLISHING

Published by Arcadia Publishing
Charleston, South Carolina

For all general information contact Arcadia Publishing at:
Telephone 843-853-2070
Fax 843-853-0044
E-mail sales@arcadiapublishing.com
For customer service and orders:
Toll-Free 1-888-313-2665

Visit us on the Internet at www.arcadiapublishing.com

Front Cover: Bert Call and Wint Fay returning from a hunting trip at Foss Pond, Kingsbury, in 1902. On the way home they had a flat tire on the 1900 Stanley Steamer and filled the tire with molasses to continue. This was the first auto in Dexter. The photograph was taken on Main Street at the present traffic light. In the background are the Abbott Memorial Library, the town hall, and the Universalist church (to the left).

PUBLIC LIBRARY, SOLDIERS MONUMENT AND TOWN HALL, DEXTER, MAINE   2184

Many consider the centerpieces of Dexter to be the Abbott Memorial Library, the Universalist church, the town hall, and the Soldiers' Monument. The monument was constructed by the local shop of Morse & Bridges for $2,000 and dedicated on July 4, 1890. The soldier is 6-feet 6-inches tall, and the overall length is 24 feet. One Dexter resident said that a popular prank for young Dexter boys during the 1930s was to shimmy up the statue and place a paper bag over the head of the soldier. You had to be tall and lanky to accomplish the feat.

Contents

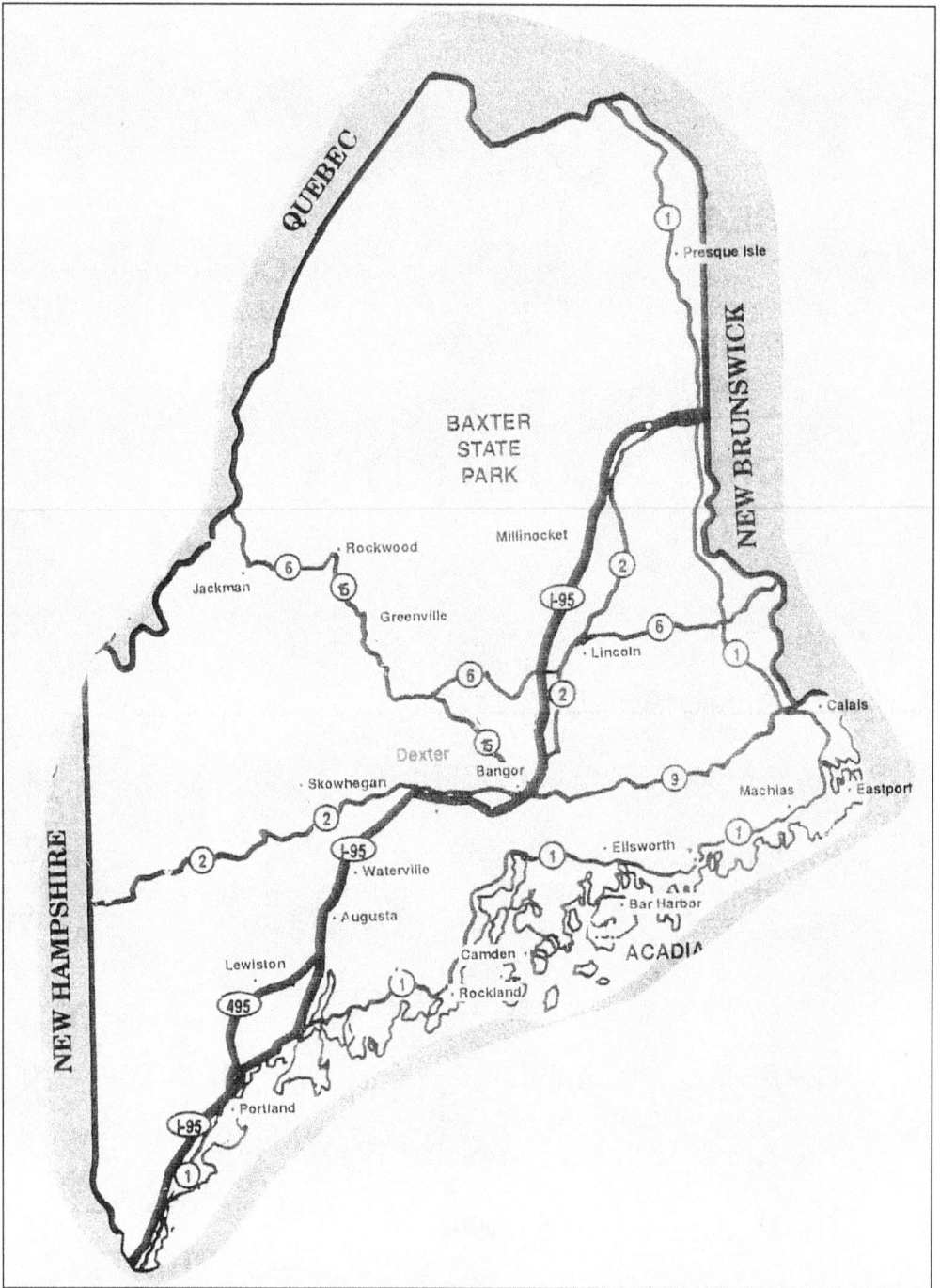

What Tim Sample thinks about Maine: "What I think is interesting about Mainers in a general sense is that we have a very high capacity for accepting reality . . . Including the vicissitudes of weather and the economy and that sort of thing . . . Mainers are not quite as shallow or superficially oriented as maybe people in some parts of the country. We've for a long time had a kind of ethic, a kind of point of view, of it's not how much money you make but what kind of human being you are that counts."

6

Introduction

"The true character of the spirit of an age is better revealed in its mode of regarding and expressing trivial and common place things than in the high manifestations of philosophy and science."

J. Huizinga, from *The Waning of The Middle Ages* (1924)

I just love these people! With all their idiosyncrasies, warmth, meanness, concern, greed, generosity—I love them. Why did I put this book together? I felt the people I have personally known for forty years and those I have read about had to be recorded. There is so much humanity to tell about. People define an age: the people who live, laugh, love, and die define an age, define a community, define Dexter. I compiled this book to tell about things that are spiritually rich and worth remembering. History tells us who we are as a people: photographs such as these help us to remember.

People who define a community: what does it mean? I sense it. I feel it. Anyone who has been away from Dexter for a period of time and has come home traveling north on Route 7 knows what I am talking about. As you pitch down the long slope and Dexter comes into view, something happens. To view the hills all around you and know what you're coming home to is a feeling unlike any other. I have tried to express it—it's always accompanied by goose bumps on the back of my neck. It's the people and their basic humanity you're coming back to. It's fragile, and it has a dark side, but it's always a welcome sight. We've got something here. This compilation of photographs from 1847 to the present is an attempt to explain it.

The photographs chosen for this publication were meant to say something—to relate a story that is part of our culture. To show the sinews of life, everyday life. To hand down the traditional heritage of rural Maine to our children and help them discover their roots.

Dexter is a community that has matured over its two hundred years but is still tied together by a common invisible thread leading back to the earliest settlers. It is a community that takes pride in itself. I want to give people a sense of continuity, to bridge a generation gap, to show how fascinating the story of ordinary life can be, and to show the spiritual bond connecting the ages.

This book is a compilation of photographs, accompanied by vignettes and anecdotes that reveal more than the photographs show. It is a guided tour divided into eight ages. Chapters one through three are a basic general historical survey. Starting in chapter four the emphasis becomes more on the people in each era that helped define the community—that gave it its distinguishing characteristics. Our heritage is built brick by brick through the decades until it becomes a solid foundation. Today we have a culture molded by many individuals, and I want the world to know these people, how they lived, and how they affected Dexter.

Like most eastern seaboard settlements, the history of central Maine and Dexter begins with European immigrants using major rivers to travel inland. The first white settlers had already begun moving north on the Penobscot and Kennebec Rivers to this area by 1800. Moving slowly inland, the first settlers arrived at the highest geographic point of land between the two rivers. Here they began settling on "the flat," below the outlet of a large lake. Today this area is known as downtown Dexter.

Early cameras were very different from modern ones, and early photographs often consist of groups of people or portraits. Almost all were posed; there are very few old photographs of people in action. Images of ordinary Maine people performing commonplace and workplace activities are rare.

An attempt has been made to use as many interesting and unforgettable photographs as possible, ones that show the local citizenry at work or play. I tried to include people from all walks of life. Many of the photographs are from the Dexter Historical Society archives and have not been seen by the public before. In addition, old albums and scrapbooks were scoured for valuable photographs. Certain people epitomize an age–some are almost legendary. Some of the photographs were taken by amateur local photographers, but most were taken by professional photographer Bert L. Call, who documented central and northern Maine for sixty-five years starting in 1886 from his studio on Main Street in Dexter.

In the following pages I have attempted to show two hundred years of "community" during both bountiful and bad times. The question is, as one observes modern life, does our present lifestyle support "community" or diminish it? You be the judge.

One

The Pioneer Age
1796–1829

When the first pioneers of Maine came to this area around 1800, this was what they saw: the Dexter hills, although they were covered with forest then. This photograph was taken from Skimmer Lane looking east toward Liberty Street and the Fay & Scott factory.

PEARSON 95

In 1814 the family of seven-year-old Maria Jennings Keene left the river town of Penobscot and trekked inland toward Dexter. According to Maria's mother "Penobscot was a drinking place where many boys grew up to follow the sea." The Jennings didn't want to chance this happening to their children, so they journeyed further inland. Maria drove a pig ahead of her during the trek, but the Jennings were forced to sell the pig in the small riverside village of Kenduskeag when it refused to be driven further.

A portrait of Maria Jennings Keene, who left a very detailed account of her family's arduous trek up the Kenduskeag River from Castine as they traveled inland to their new home in Elkinstown (Dexter). Along the way Maria found herself shoeless when they were burned by a misplaced hot kettle. Maria spoke often of how she, her five brothers, and the neighboring children were shoeless in the central Maine wilderness, a great irony since her father was a cobbler.

Dexter's first settlers arrived in 1800. Ebenezer Small and his family were the first to clear land, raise a crop, and build a dwelling—a brush camp on the hillside across from the present Annie's Restaurant on Main Street. Mrs. Small was actively involved in the difficult life that pioneers here faced; while her husband was away one day, she found a bear in one of his traps, killed it, dragged it home, and dressed it out. She had the bear meat cooked and ready for Ebenezer's supper when he returned that night.

PEARSON 45

Aphia Small was one of the first children born in Dexter. Her sister Joannah was the first white child born here. These girls grew up and watched their father move from the camp on Main Street to Zion's Hill, build a house, and plant an orchard. Ebenezer and his son built a dam and sawmill near the modern site of the Brick Mill (presently Dexter Shoe Company's No. 1 shop on Water Street). Aphia married Abel Abbott, and their son, Peter Amos Abbott, was the grandfather of Ruth Dudley, who currently lives on Forest Street.

11

When entrepreneur Jonathan Farrar (1771–1838) came from Bloomfield (Skowhegan) in 1817, he bought this house on the Main Street hill and ran the first store and post office in the front portion. He bought saw, grist, and carding mills in the area, dug a canal and mill pond, began a grist mill on the site of the present museum in downtown Dexter, and soon began a tannery (later Shaws). In 1835 he began a woolen mill with Lysander Cutler that eventually became Dumbarton Mill. He also donated land for a common (the present skating rink), and the land for the Universalist church. The telephone company building is now on the site of this house.

The Greene Tavern was built about 1819 by Deacon Benjamin Greene on upper Main Street, where travelers from Bangor would enter town. Early town meetings were held here as well as social gatherings. It was later moved around the corner, where it still stands, on the Charleston Road.

Records of cattle and sheep marks, from the first *Dexter Town Book*. Early settlers used a common pasture and needed a way to identify their own sheep.

The Bates Tavern, completed by John Bates in 1822 on lower Main Street near the base of Zion's Hill, served travelers arriving from the west. Bates also had a store and was the first town clerk and a selectman. The first town library was housed in a cupboard in the tavern. The building was moved to Ripley by Fred Tibbetts in 1913 to make way for the present Wayside Park.

In 1820, two brothers came to Dexter in search of a mill site. Amos and Jeremiah Abbott visited numerous sites Downeast before deciding to purchase the mill and privilege of Jonathan Farrar. Eventually, two of their other brothers followed them to Dexter, Joshua and Paschal, and a fifth, Abel, lived here for a short time before returning to Andover, Massachusetts. This picture of the five brothers had to have been taken between 1847 (when Paschal moved here) and 1859 (when Paschal died). In 1894, when George Amos Abbott, son of Amos Abbott, donated a library building to the town, he dedicated the structure to the four brothers who lived out their lives here: Amos, Jeremiah, Joshua, and Paschal. From left to right are: (front row) Abel, Paschal, and Jeremiah; (back row) Amos and Joshua. One interesting side note concerning Amos and Jeremiah: they married sisters, daughters of Lieutenant John Safford. Amos married Mehitable and Jeremiah married Lucy Safford.

The Amos Abbott & Company Mill at the outlet of Pleasant Pond, now Lake Wassookeag. This business was begun by Amos and Jeremiah Abbott in 1820, when they purchased the mill site, buildings, and water privilege from Jonathan Farrar. At the time of the purchase by the Abbotts the site contained a sawmill and carding mill. By 1836 the mill was fully integrated, manufacturing woolen cloth from raw wool to finished product. The Abbotts always claimed that the mill was the first fully-integrated woolen mill in the state of Maine.

Nathaniel Bryant was one of Dexter's most successful early farmers. In 1845 he operated 4 farms, and by 1848 he kept 900 sheep and 5 pair of oxen. During the 1850s he reduced his sheep herd and by 1853 he had only 250 sheep. His focus turned more and more to dairy cows; he owned 56 by 1853, and churning butter became a big business. The butter was churned by horse power, and it is said that he employed "a Dutch dairy maid from Pennsylvania, who had a plump and sturdy figure, strong white arms and good hands for butter making." Mt. Pleasant Cemetery was created from his lands on Bryant Hill.

Nathaniel Bryant
1808 - 1863

15

"A man who wore many hats." Lysander Cutler was one of the key individuals who helped to develop the town's industrial base during the antebellum era. He arrived in Dexter in 1828 from Massachusetts with just $2 in his pocket. In two years he was a partner with the Abbotts and in 1836 he started his own mill, eventually operating three woolen mills in Dexter. He started the Dexter Rifle Company in 1835 and the fire department a year later. He led the Dexter men to Aroostook County during the Aroostook War and served as a town selectman and a representative to the legislature. The Panic of 1857 ruined him and he went west. At the outbreak of the Civil War he organized a regiment in Wisconsin and attained the rank of brigadier general. He died in 1866 in Milwaukee from complications due to his wounds.

Lysander Cutler's home, located on lower Main Street across from the Stone or Dumbarton Mill. The building was razed during the 1980s.

Two

The Antebellum Age
1830–1859

Main Street looking east from Zion's Hill, 1846. This photograph is one of the earliest Main Street photographs known to exist in the state of Maine. The original daguerreotype was reproduced in the early 1900s by longtime photographer Bert Call. (The original was later stolen from the town's library in the late 1970s.) The picture appears to have been taken during a snow or rainstorm. The old Dexter House (left) served as a hotel from 1846 to 1876. The building has the distinction of being moved twice. The steepled building in the upper left is the Universalist church; built in 1829, it was Dexter's first church. Directly right of the Universalist church and in the middle of Main Street is the Eaton Store, which years later became known as the T&K (Thurston & Kingsbury) Store. It was razed in 1949 to make room for a filling station, and is now the site of the Dexter Oil Company. The building in the top center with the cupola was Dexter's first town hall, which collapsed during the town meeting of 1856. It was purchased by the Abbotts, moved, and incorporated into their mill complex. Dr. Burleigh's home (to the right from the town hall) is currently the site of the Abbott Memorial Library. The home was moved in 1894 to make room for the new library.

Reuben Flanders was born in Cornville, Maine, in 1811, and moved to Dexter when he was nineteen years old. In 1856 he invented a machine for cutting stock for the manufacture of orange and lemon crates, which he never patented. He engaged in the manufacture of cutting stock for crates in a building known as "the old boxmill" in the lower part of the town. (The site of the mill was next to the dam of the Dexter Shoe Company's No. 1 shop on Liberty Street.) In 1867 he purchased a mill in North Dexter and moved his lemon and orange crate business there. He also extensively manufactured long and short lumber.

Witherell's Island was the farm home of Reverend Joseph F. Witherell. Witherell founded our present newspaper, *The Eastern Gazette*, on March 12, 1853. It was first called *The Gem and Gazette*. Mr. Witherell complained often about the difficulty in obtaining quality paper. His small farming operation required that he stop publication of the paper a few weeks every summer to do his haying. He had sheep that roamed this island for many years.

"So, what is Maine? It is an attitude, a way of life, and the last democracy. It is a place where most people refer to their elected representatives by their first name. We send people to Augusta and Washington named Margaret, Ed, Joe, Jock, Bill, George, and Olympia, and when they go there they work and vote for cleaner air and cleaner politics. Maine people are in credibly independent. We like to claim that we "do as we please." And we do, but we do not bother other people when we do it. We are also very loving and caring people. We reject the spurious, the faker, and the fraud. Steve and Tabitha King walk the streets with everyone else, give money to charity without publicity, and turn Maine folk tales into modern black humor and no one pays any particular attention to them. They are simply Maine people. We still do business with a handshake, mostly always with other Mainers, still can see fraud or ethical violation when it appears, and live our lives rejoicing that we are not 'from away.' "

Professor David C. Smith, from the January 26, 1990 edition of the *Maine Times*

Improved Horizontal

Hand Drilling Machine,

——FOR——

BLACKSMITHS, CARRIAGE MAKERS, MILLMEN, AND GENERAL USE.

WHOLE WEIGHT, 120 LBS.

24 Inch Balance Wheel weighs 60 lbs.

Length of Bed, 2 Feet 8 Inches.

Extreme Distance between Spindle and Rest, 13 Inches.

Swings 12 Inches.

Steel Feed Screws.

Feeds 3 Inches.

Arbors, 1 1-8 Inches.

Can be arranged to be used by Foot or Power.

N. Dustin & Co., Dexter, Me.,

MANUFACTURERS.

Nathaniel Dustin (1814–1890). Mr. Dustin developed a foundry and machine shop near the present Reny's store. In the 1840s the foundry's owners became involved in a long-running feud with the Grist Mill's owners over the amount of water they needed to run their businesses. As technology improved, more water was needed than could be provided by the normal flow of the stream. One day Mr. Dustin's business partner George Fitzgerald was in the water at the junction of the stream and mill pond, when Warren Carr from the Grist Mill showed up. "He threatened to put me in the stream and I threatened to put him in. I told him we should take it every time under same circumstances." This was the statement Mr. Fitzgerald said under oath at the eventual trial over the water rights on Main Street. In 1883 the feud was finally resolved in favor of the Grist Mill. In 1887, N. Dustin & Co. moved their business to Oakland, Maine.

By 1818 post roads were opened between Skowhegan, Dexter, and Bangor. At first the mail was carried by post riders. By 1822 a two-horse covered carriage was used for the mail and passengers, driven by Lawrence Green. John Favor had a Troy coach he used on the road between Dexter and Skowhegan. By the 1840s a route from Waterville through Dexter to Greenville was established. Jere MacDonald was the regular stagecoach driver later on and is shown here driving the stage in the 1901 centennial celebration. When the 1951 celebration was being planned, Erma Bentley looked for this stagecoach to use again in the parade. Much to her dismay, she found that after the 1901 celebration it was stored outdoors behind a barn someplace in the #10 District and was no longer usable.

Dexter has always had its share of musicians. One of the first was Joshua Berry, who cleared the land out on Bement Hill going toward Ripley where the Wintle family now lives. By the Civil War, Dexter had a band of its own, and was justly proud of its musicians. In the above photograph the old Dexter band of 1868 poses in the middle of Main Street in front of what is now Annie's Restaurant (right) and the site of Reny's (in the background). From left to right are: Frank Campbell, Horace Grant, Charles Flanagan, Bob France, leader Dick Shaw, John Dickson, Tom Knowles, Stillman Mason, John Crossland, John Campbell, and Reuban Taylor.

Tom Rodgers was considered a mechanical genius by many in town. In 1860 he designed a 57-foot-long stone bridge to go across the narrows of the lake and replace the floating bridge, which had mysteriously gotten loose from its mooring along the north shore. The first floating bridge, built in 1824, was constructed of logs, heavy timbers, and planks, and was secured at either shore with self-adjusting inclines of about 35 feet. Where the inclines rested on the float there was about 25 feet covered with water. In 1828 it was voted at the town meeting to "pay Royal Copeland for sundry articles lost by his father in passing over the floating bridge." There was a second floating bridge built in 1844, before the stone bridge was built in 1860, at a cost of $4,000. At the 1883 town meeting the town voted to "raise the passage between the upper and lower lake so that boats can pass through." A timber framed tower was built above the bridge and the "draw" was operated by the person desiring to pass from one pond to the other. In 1935 the bridge was widened to 35 feet, regraveled, and tarred. The draws were replanked with 3-by-6-foot timbers on edge over steel beams. Later a Tarvia mat was placed over the planking. In 1947 the present concrete bridge was built.

Thomas Rogers
1815–187_

Relegated to a corner of Bailey's garage, this Eagle 3 hand tub was overlooked when the call went out for scrap metal during World War II. It had been purchased by Dexter in 1836 and used regularly until 1920, when the fire department was motorized with the arrival of a La France truck. Dexter had used five of these hand tubs at one time. The Eagle has been used as a parade piece for the last forty-five years. It has a special nozzle that throws a 1-inch stream of water 185 feet. The total capacity is about 150 gallons, and takes about 5 minutes to pump out. Usually the crew consists of at least fourteen men, with six men pumping on the breaks on each side. When it is loaded it weighs around 3,000 pounds. Vern Bodwell rebuilt much of its wood structure and the wheels were rebuilt in Massachusetts. At the Maine Federation of Fire Fighters convention a few years ago the East Corinth Fire Department challenged the Dexter Fire Department to a race around the track in Skowhegan. Dexter was up to the challenge and won before a large crowd. What made the race unusual was that East Corinth's rig was being pulled by ponies.

RESIDENCE OF JOB ABBOTT.

RESIDENCE OF GEORGE A. ABBOTT.

An illustration of the Amos Abbott & Company Mill complex and homes from the 1882 *History of Penobscot County*. The building on the lower left in the mill complex was originally the Dexter Town Hall. The floor collapsed during the town meeting in 1856, dropping three hundred residents to the basement. Miraculously no one was really hurt except the sheriff, who landed on the hot barrel woodstove. His exclamations were said to be very vigorous. The building was bought by the Abbott brothers, moved, repaired, and used for offices. It still stands nearly across from the Universalist church. Both residences pictured are gone; their sites are now occupied by Bud's Shop N' Save.

The woolen industry played an important part in Dexter's growth from 1830 to 1860. During that time six different woolen factories were constructed. Three are pictured here: the White Mill (upper left), the "Brick" or Union Mill (upper right), and the Stone or Dunbarton Mill (bottom). The White Mill was first constructed in 1842 as a grist mill by the Abbott brothers. In 1846 it was purchased by the firm of Farrar & Cutler, who added 80 feet to the structure and had the building operating as a woolen factory in 90 days. The mill was located at the intersection of Mill and Water Streets, and burned during a spectacular fire in July 1940. The "Brick" Mill or Union Mill, now Dexter Shoe Company's No. 1 shop, was constructed in 1848 by the firm of Foss & Conant. It was added to extensively and became the home of the Dexter Shoe Company in 1957, when they located in Dexter. The Stone or Dunbarton Mill was constructed in 1844 by Farrar & Cutler to replace their mill that burned the previous year. The two bottom stories were made of stone quarried in Dexter and two stories of wood were later added on in 1867. The mill was razed in 1974 and is now the site of the Chia Apartments.

Three

The Gilded Age 1860–1889

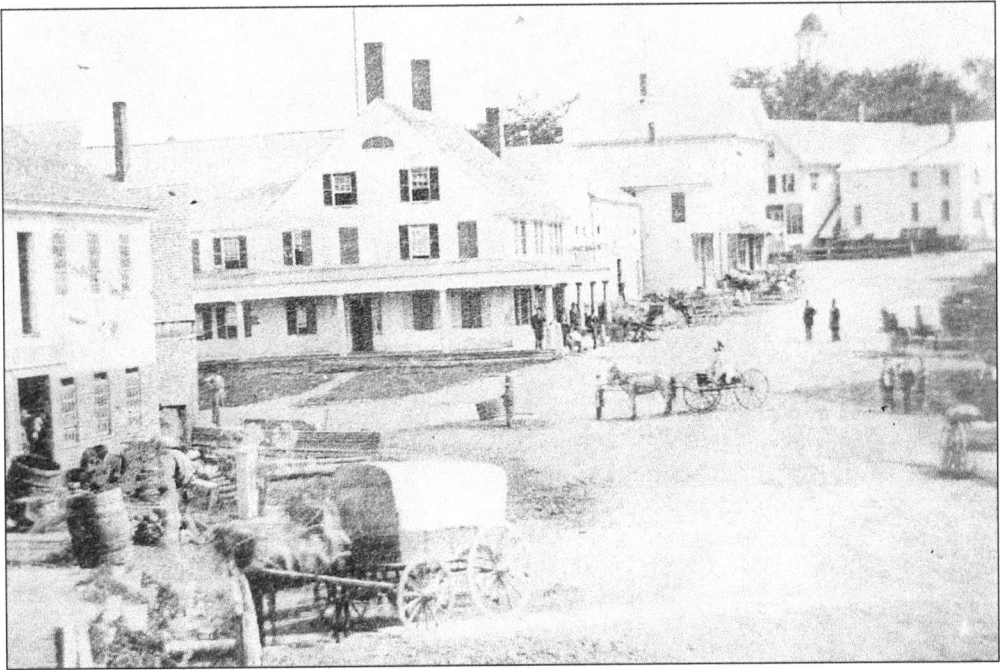

Dexter's Main Street, 1865. This section of Main Street was always referred to as "the flat" during the 1800s and early 1900s. The Dexter House, the large building with the porch in the center of the picture, was later picked up and moved one lot down in 1876 to make room for the new Bank Block. It stayed there until 1906 when again it was moved to lower Main Street and converted to a tenement building. Note the granite crosswalk in the foreground, used by pedestrians to cross the muddy streets. A little boy is standing next to the town's waterpump just below the Dexter House, and the couple in the buckboard seem to be posing for the photographer. The Universalist church steeple can be seen in the background, but the remainder of the church is obstructed by trees. The Universalist church went through a major renovation in 1869, when the present steeple was constructed.

Five members of the 6th Battery Maine Artillery Volunteers who enlisted together in 1864. From left to right are: Daniel Dolloff Jr., Samuel Morrill, Gancelo Safford, George P. Toward, and Henry L. Wood. Dexter contributed heavily during the Civil War, with 235 men from town enlisting to serve the Union. Thirty-eight men died or were killed in action. Thirty-six men from Dexter served in the 6th Maine Infantry Volunteers alone, the most in any one unit. One individual who seemed to illustrate the feeling of patriotism of the day was Simon A. Abbott. A grandson of Dexter's first settler, Ebenezer Small, Simon enlisted in the 12th Maine Infantry on December 15, 1861, but by December became severely ill and was discharged as disabled. He returned to Dexter to convalesce, and it seemed the war was over for him. He had volunteered to serve, but his service had been cut short by circumstances beyond his control. Simon apparently had time to reflect on his circumstances and felt he had not done enough, for on February 29, 1864, he reenlisted, this time in the 6th Maine Artillery Volunteers. Whether he was fully recovered from his illness is unknown, but he may have felt that his debt to his nation was unfulfilled and there was a strong need or feeling of duty to prove his patriotism. Whatever drove Simon Abbott to reenlist may never be known, but it cost him his life, as he was mortally wounded at Cold Harbor, Virginia, and died on June 5, 1864.

28

"Scene on the Owlsboro Road opposite Les Cousin's. Left to right: David Gilman, and Hookey, Fred Bailey with team. Near center: Will Hayden and Ira Hayes. Back of Ira Hayes: Mr. Booker. At right of Mr. Booker: a little back his eight children. Two women sitting down: Mrs. Bagley and Mrs. Hersey. Drilling rock: Abner Starbird. This picture was in the clearing of this land which developed in a nice field and a large barn was soon built to house the hay and crops by Will Hayden." The above was written on the back of this photograph. It was found in Rosa Pendexter's home on Dustin Street in 1970 and is presently in the files of the Dexter Historical Society. This site is near Ted Dube's camp on the Owlsboro Road.

A rumor heard often in Dexter throughout the years, although never confirmed, is that there is an Italian immigrant worker buried in the trestle at Lincoln Street. We do know that Italian laborers from Boston were brought here to build the railroad north. Even today some of the old-timers from the #10 District remember hearing about "Little Italy," a parcel of land owned by Florence Turek's great grandfather, Dr. Orlando Mellon Robinson, and located just beyond Lizzie Newcomb's farm in the #10 District. The railroad was chartered in 1867 to come to Dexter from Newport. The towns of Corinna and Dexter used their credit to finance the project. Dexter raised $225,000 and Corinna $75,000. The first depot was on Railroad Avenue and Liberty Street. In 1889 the railroad was extended to Dover-Foxcroft and went through Silver's Mills. The coming of the railroad had a major economic impact on the town. The industries, especially the woolen mills, were able to receive raw wool and transport finished products much more efficiently and cheaply. Passenger services allowed the people of Dexter to become more mobile. This opportunity to travel may be one reason that Dexter's population dropped from 1870 to 1880 by 312, to 2,563.

"The Italian, who has perambulated Dexter Streets and peddled ice cream this season, had his foot crushed while working at rail laying near Silver's Mills Tuesday last. The troller or handcar ran onto his foot, pinching one side of it under the wheel much as the accident to the boy James Martine had last week occurred. Dr. Thatcher attended him. His name is John Russ." This article, which appeared in the August 30, 1889 edition of *The Eastern State*, reveals the difficulty and pain involved in bringing the railroad to Dexter.

Built in 1866 by Loring Hayes, the Exchange Hotel stood for many years between Main Street and the post office. It had many owners in its time but none more colorful than Del Cleveland and his dog Grover. The story goes that local folk at the Exchange would flip a nickel into Grover's mouth and open the door. Grover would run to Jim Kerby's store, where Jim would take the nickel and place a package of lozenges in his mouth. Grover would then faithfully run back to the hotel and deposit his package to the delight of all present, who would then give Grover one for his reward.

This photograph hung on the office wall of Abbott's Mill for many years. Information regarding the location of the photograph and the people involved has proved impossible to obtain.

Dexter High School class of 1896.

1883			
Jan 13	"	Comb Brush	15
Mar 20	"	1 Rob't Brush	50
" "	"	Rp Harness	85
Apr 10	"	Piece Rubber Cloth	20
May 23	"	Rp Reins	10

An 1883 billhead from the harness business of William Judson Haseltine to Job Abbott, featuring an interesting vignette of a horse, sulky, and driver. W.J. Haseltine is first mentioned as a harness maker in 1879 at the foot of Zion's Hill in a building known as the Old Tavern, and he was still in business as late as 1920, despite the popularity of the automobile. William died in 1932 as a result of a "shock of paralysis." Many Dexter residents will remember his granddaughter, Ruth Haseltine, a photographer for many years in Dexter who was best remembered for taking class pictures in the Dexter school system.

An 1873 billhead of the J.H. Gould & Co. to Job Abbott. John H. Gould, a dealer in meats and vegetables, began his business in 1871 at the southeast corner of Main and Spring Streets in the Allen Merrill Building, now the site of the post office. Following the Civil War, there was a sizeable increase in the number of small businesses. This increase in the number of businesses and the specialization of these businesses illustrates a heightened prosperity in the town of Dexter. One important factor in Dexter's increased prosperity was the building of the railroad from Newport to Dexter in 1869.

FITZGERALD'S
IMPROVED INVIGORATOR

Cures all Diseases of the Blood as it Works Directly Upon the Blood.

It will cure Pimples, Boils, Carbuncles, Humors, Scrofula, White Swelling, Running Sores, Tumors, Cancers, Salt Rheum, Eczema, Erysipelas, Canker, Rheumatism, Neuralgia, Headache, Catarrh, Dyspepsia, Loss of Appetite, General Debility, Nervousness, and in short all Stomach, Liver and Kidney Complaints.

Fitzgerald's Improved Invigorator

Is prepared solely by FITZGERALD & CO., at the Medical Home Laboratory in Allston, Mass, It can be found on Sale at Wholesale and Retail Druggists.

PRICE $1.00 PER BOTTLE. SIX BOTTLES FOR $5.00

An advertisement for Dr. Orrin Fitzgerald Jr., a spiritualist healer in Dexter from the time of the Civil War until his death in 1897. Orrin came to Dexter at the age of five from Caanan, Maine. Very early on his parents noticed his unusual spiritual powers, which were an embarrassment to the family, and they shipped young Orrin off to the "wilds of Garland" to live with a spiritualist by the name of Jonathan Lawrence. Under Jonathan's tutelage, Orrin learned to control his unusual abilities. The spirit that controlled his body was an Indian spirit by the name of William Lybush, and it stayed with Orrin all his life. Upon making a diagnosis, Orrin would go into a trance and the Indian spirit would effect the cure. When he came out from under the influence of the spirit, the doctor would always ask, "What did the Old Indian tell you?" Dr. Fitzgerald bottled his Improved Invigorator and a Membrane Cure in a laboratory on lower Main Street on the site of Gary's Garage today. He also maintained a medical home in Allston, Massachusetts, and spent time between both places. This advertisement was printed in *The Eastern State* newspaper, a Dexter weekly paper started and owned by Dr. Fitzgerald in 1888 in the Advent Building on the corner of Pleasant and Main Streets.

Dr. Fitzgerald at the reins of his medicine wagon in front of the Snell House in Houlton, Maine. The doctor traveled throughout the state and kept office hours in other communities regularly. The unusual hitch of four horses in single file is of special interest, and the wagon is lettered, advertising his "Improved Invigorator." One story in particular has survived regarding the doctors travels. While boarding the train at the station in Skowhegan, Dr. Fitzgerald was approached by a man and a young girl who asked for his help. The young girl had a growth on her eyelid, and after making appropriate apologies, the doctor asked the train to be held for two minutes. Before a crowd of witnesses on the station platform Dr. Fitzgerald removed a scalpel from his bag, closed his eyes, and removed the tumor. The young lady remarked afterward that she hardly felt a thing. Dr. Fitzgerald also had a fancy carriage for his private use, which was used by the city of Bangor to convey President U.S. Grant in a parade. It was said to be one of the finest around. Dr. Fitzgerald had a reputation of being ostentatious and many seemed to think he flaunted his wealth.

The home of Dr. Orrin Fitzgerald Jr., located on lower Main Street next to the Crosby-Neal Funeral Home, as it appeared in the 1930s to 1940s. Built in 1870 at a reported cost of $60,000, Dr. Fitzgerald spared no cost in constructing one of the finest houses in eastern Maine. Directly in front of the house was a 2.5-foot-tall iron statue of a black boy. Stopping there the doctor would press a button in the statue's chest and a bell would ring in the stable to summon the hostler to come and get the horses. A popular fourth of July prank was to dump a can of red paint over the statue, which prompted a later owner to hire a guard to watch over it.

When winter arrived wagons and carriages were put away in favor of sleighs and pungs. Snow on the streets was packed down by snowrollers (like the one above) to facilitate traveling via runners. Raymond Whitney Sr. remembers that when the first snow began to fly, cars were blocked up in the barn with the tires off the floor. All fluids were drained from the vehicles, and the valve cover gaskets and valves were removed. The operation was reversed in the late spring, when the valves were reground and replaced, fluids refilled, tires remounted, and the car was taken off the blocks. With the plowing of winter roads this process became unnecessary.

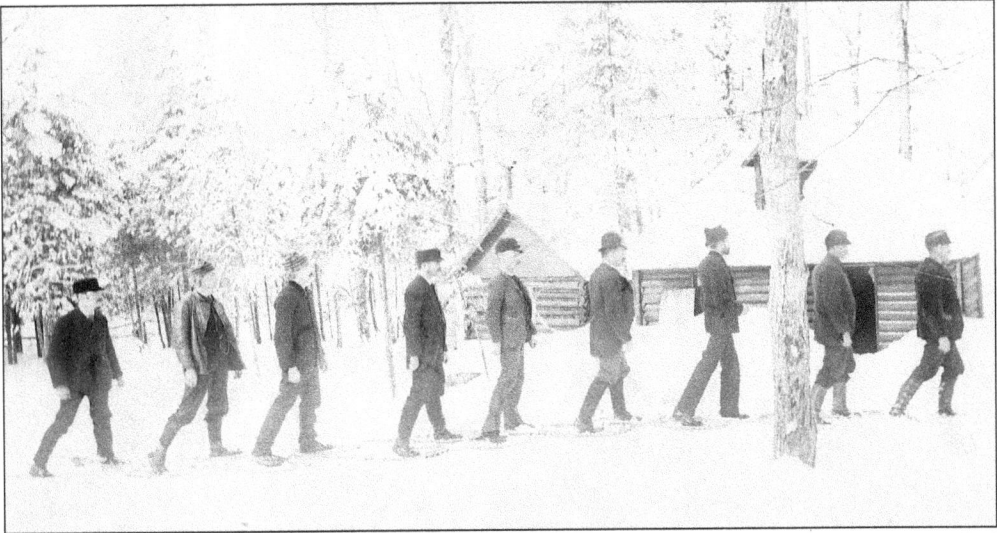

The Wanalancett Snowshoe Club was a familiar sight in Dexter in the 1880s. Bert Call recalled that during the great snowstorm of 1888, while he was in the living room of his future wife's home at night and observing the storm out the window, this club came down the middle of Spring Street with torches lighting the way. Pictured are, from left to right: John DuBourdieu, Will Haines, Dr. Haines, Ed Russ, Wes Judkins, Elmer Brewster, Arthur Abbott, Peter Abbott, and Stan Leighton.

Standing for many years where the present Dexter Shoe Camps are on Lake Wassookeag was the "Moosehorn" log cabin. One of the earliest recreational buildings on the lake, it was eventually torn down when the summer school camp was established. From left to right are: (front row) John DuBourdieu, tailor; Will Haines, town clerk; Charles Favor, harness maker; Dr. Charles Haines, dentist; N.H. Fay, machine shop; Sam Small, Grist Mill; Wes Judkins, insurance; and V. Macomber, meats; (back row) Will Brewster, groceries; Forrest Parsons, groceries; Peter Amos Abbott, fish and furs; Stan Leighton, bank; Elmer Brewster, drug store; and Warren Carr, hardware.

"The score stood 93 to 41 and it was supposed to be good baseball, too!!" This was the headline from the June 15, 1874 edition of a Dover newspaper after the Dover team, the Resolutes, were defeated in a five-hour game in Dover by the Dexter White Caps. The White Caps were Dexter's first baseball team. Organized in 1871, they played twenty games through 1874 and were victorious most of the time, frequently in games with scores in double figures.

Maine has always had a "mud season." This is Church Street in front of Bud's Shop and Save, before road or sidewalk paving. But Dexter was trying to improve conditions, as indicated by the following warrants for the 1894 Town Meeting: Article 62—To see if the town will change the sidewalk on Free Street from a plank sidewalk to a concrete sidewalk; Article 52—To see if the town will vote to build a concrete walk from the Grange Hall door down to Main Street.

Fannie Brackett Damon (1875–1939) was a graduate of Castine Normal and a teacher before marrying L.R. Damon. She edited two literary magazines that achieved national notice: *The Quiet Hours* (1887–1889) and *The Tally Ho* (1896–1899). Poetry was her strongest means of self-expression, and it reveals her awareness of the beauties of both God and nature—New England style.

The Return

An old brown fence, a bramble hedge, A strip of snow, a pasture ledge,
A rugged bank, a sluggish drain, A rick of stones, a drowsy rain.
I look and laugh: a thrill of hope Shoots through me from the bramble slope.
For all the colors that have died Shall come again intensified.
A little hence the buds shall start And open fling their joyous heart,
And come so fast, and come so sweet The birds shall fly from far retreat
To keep with bloom a singing pace And all but perish in the race.
The thrifty ants shall hither run, Bees haste and hum from sun to sun,
Yet none be able to draw up The honey from a honey-cup.

Eagle Hose Company No. 1, the French company, posed for this photograph on the Pleasant Street School grounds during the late 1800s. Pictured here are, from left to right: (front row) ? Bertrand, Peter Mountain, Edward Mountain, and Zeb Pomroy; (middle row) Harry Dyer, John Ronco, Edward Clukey, and Elmer Clukey; (back row) Charles Mountain, Frank Clukey, Charles Clukey, Charles Dulac, and Joe Mountain. Most of the men lived in close proximity of the school grounds, mostly on Pleasant and Grove Streets.

"For many years, in fact there has hardly been a time when A.L. Barton, who resides in the east part of Dexter, has not been able to count among his possessions one pair of oxen at least which was a little larger than any to be found elsewhere in that part of the state. The larger one of the yoke tips the scale at 2,900, pounds is exactly nine feet long from the roots of his horn to the roots of his tail. The other is not as large but girts eight feet four inches. The pair weighs 5,580 pounds."

from *The Eastern Gazette*

40

The Barton District has a rich and interesting history and played a major role in Dexter's early development. In 1802 the site of the barn pictured above, which still stands, was the early settlement homestead of Seba French and his family. The story goes that after Mr. Barton purchased this property he decided to build the biggest barn in Dexter. At that time Charles Shaw had the largest one, located where Hamp Crouse farmed for many years on the Ripley Road. Barton's barn was reportedly bigger than Shaw's barn (which burned in 1963) by a few feet.

Of all the lovely elms that once graced the streets of Dexter (before the Dutch Elm disease), this one at the foot of Zion's Hill held the warmest spot in everyone's heart. In fact, when Tommy Bickell's nearby store caught on fire around 1874, the firemen turned the hose on the tree and let the store burn. The tree was set out in 1837 by a group of businessmen including Lysander Cutler, Nat Dustin, and Hiram Bassett, and was still standing in the 1940s.

41

Elijah Sprague was induced by offers of land to bring his blacksmithing talents to the "French district" of Dexter in 1803. His son, Volney Sprague (1817–1908), practiced as a lawyer in Dexter for twenty-six years; perhaps his best service, however, was in recording verbal accounts of Dexter's history, which he wrote up over the years to give us much of what we now know of Dexter's past.

V. A. Sprague

"Henry Glass came to Dexter in 1839. He was a plain-spoken, honest-hearted, whole-souled man, fearful of nothing but sin; always ready to help in any good cause; never hesitating to rebuke unrighteousness. He was dearly beloved by his church associates, and honored by them as their Steward, Trustee, Class Leader and Treasurer. He died on the 13th of June, 1890. Leaving no children he willed his property to the church he loved."

Hiram A. Keene, from the *History of the Methodist Episcopal Church* (1822–1900)

The year: 1871. The place: the new tomb at Mount Pleasant Cemetery. The event: Deacon Henry Glass got locked in the tomb. The story, as related by Erma Bentley in March 1970, went like this: "Dr. Ryan's father and a crew of men were working on the new tomb at the cemetery and prepared to leave after a days work. Deacon Glass stayed on after everyone left to finish up when a gust of wind slammed the door shut. There weren't any door handles on the inside because anyone in a tomb wouldn't have any need to get out. Well, Deacon Glass commenced to howl, scream, cry, moan, and shout. Mr. Ryan forgot something and had to go back up the hill. When he approached the tomb he said he heard sounds like he never heard before coming from the small vent at the top of the tomb. When he opened the door the Deacon fell out prostrate on the ground. Mr. Ryan loaded him on his wagon of tools and drove down to the Glass residence on Spring Street near Lincoln Street and dumped the Deacon on the lawn. Mrs. Glass came out, saw her husband lying on the lawn still in a state of shock, and proclaimed, 'Why didn't the old fool keep still; I knew where he was.' Rumor has it that the Deacon's hair turned grey that day."

43

"Old Fannie" is shown here with the meat cart from Frank R. Curtis' meat market, in the days before refrigeration or sanitation, about 1870. The shop was one of several meat markets that occupied this store on Grove Street, in the basement of the store built by Jonathan Farrar in 1835 (which also went through several owners). At this point it was Jenkins & Hill grocers. The Dexter Oil Company occupies this spot now.

The old Town Farm as it looks today, west of Dexter on Route 23 (which was once a stagecoach line from Skowhegan). The site still sports an rugged, hewn, weatherworn old farmhouse that protects inhabitants from the elements and beckons the curious to come closer. The homestead has kept the main features of the original Town Farm and houses the current owners, Fred and Carol Sherburne. They may still hear the whispers of secrets long kept about what happened on top of that windswept knoll over on the Ripley Road just short of the turn of the century. The farm's secrets could have been whispered by many of the people spoken of in the adjacent photograph.

44

The Town Farm as it appeared in 1897, shortly after a scandal that implicated Samuel Murphy and his wife of abusing and possibly murdering their wards. Sewell Blake, Mrs. Lovejoy, Charles Howard, and Mrs. Berry all died under suspicious circumstances atop that windy knoll on the outskirts of town during the years 1875–1881. Several local citizens testified against the Murphys. According to Mary L. Rollins: "Mrs. Lovejoy complained of ill treatment . . . I also saw Mrs. Safford, at one time, with her head bleeding, and learned that Mrs. Murphy struck her with a long-handle dipper." Mrs. Sovina Grover testified: "Mrs. Lovejoy was unwell Saturday and on Sunday did not get up during the day. In the afternoon she wanted something and Murphy called her a damned lazy bitch and told her to get up and get it herself. About nine o'clock Mrs. Murphy came to me and said Mrs. Lovejoy was dying. I went in to see her, and she did not appear to be dying, Her pulse was strong. Mrs. Murphy wanted me to give her some tea that was there in a cup. Mrs. Lovejoy did not want to take it, and I refused to give it to her. Mrs. Murphy went in and made her drink it. In two hours she was dead. Her pulse was strong till a few minutes before she died. I believe she was helped out of the world. Mrs. Lovejoy thought the tea was poisoned, and wanted to know if she should drink it and go peacefully." Formal charges were never brought against the Murphys and they returned to their family home of Mars Hill under a dark cloud of suspicion.

Honorable Josiah Crosby (1816–1904), the son of Oliver and Harriet Crosby. Born in Dover, N.H., the Honorable Josiah Crosby was a very prominent barrister who practiced his trade in Dexter for some sixty years. Crosby was schooled at Foxcroft Academy and later graduated from Bowdoin College in the Class of 1835. His name comes up in every noted legal dispute in Dexter for over a half century, including: the Barron murder, the Express Office burglary, and the Town Farm scandal.

John Wilson Barron was murdered during the well-known Dexter Savings Bank robbery of 1878. Barron was treasurer of the bank and was working on a holiday when he was killed by a robber or robbers. Although several notorious crooks of the day were rounded up, arrested, and even charged, no one was ever convicted of the crime.

This was the site of the 1878 Eastern Express Company office robbery, where $4,000 was stolen from the safe just one month before the Barron murder. A local cabinetmaker named Arthur Annett, whose airtight alibi was that he was asleep in bed with his wife at the time of the burglary, was accused early on. Mr. Annett, with the very able assistance of prominent lawyer Josiah Crosby, was eventually discharged of any wrongdoing. One eloquent Crosby argument on Annett's behalf follows: "An attempt has been made to fasten this crime on a fellow citizen of our town, a man who has sustained an unquestionable character . . . If a man of our town has been guilty of this crime, we want him ousted, but we don't want an innocent man convicted of a crime of which he is not guilty. There are a good many others who could be brought here beside Mr. Annett, against whom suspicious circumstances could be brought to bear . . . It has been claimed that no one could make the key with which the safe was opened lest he be a skilled mechanic. It is a very simple operation; there are hundreds in this house who could make one as good—could even do it myself." No one was ever convicted for this robbery and it remains an unsolved mystery to this day.

J.W. Barron was found handcuffed, gagged, and left to die with a rope around his neck. He died shortly after being discovered, lying against the vault door, unconscious. The gag was a short piece of wood taken from the bail of a water pail, and was secured by a cord passed through a hole in the wood.

Oliver Cromwell (shown here) was implicated along with David Stain in the Barron murder. Stain and Cromwell spent thirteen years in jail before being found innocent of the charges, which were brought about largely by stories made up by Stain's vindictive son. Cromwell was represented by an inexperienced public defender named Lewis Barker, who tried to prove that Barron committed suicide. Both Cromwell and Stain were eventually pardoned by Governor Powers.

David L. Stain, one of several suspects accused of murdering John Wilson Barron. Stain's son, enraged over his father's refusal to spring him from a jail in Norridgewock for crimes of his own, swore that the ghost of Barron had appeared to him and implicated his father along with Oliver Cromwell in the notorious robbery and murder. The lust for revenge apparently began shortly after the elder Stain not only refused to send bail money to his son, but apparently wrote a letter to his son saying, "I am not surprised, nor do I waste tears that you are in jail where you belong. Rather than send you money to obtain your freedom, I would send you a rope so you could hang yourself." The elder Stain was arrested in Massachusetts (where he lived at the time), and along with his implicated friend Cromwell were brought to Maine for trial in 1887.

FRIDAY, MARCH 1, 1878.

Robbery & Murder
IN DEXTER.

DEXTER SAVINGS BANK ENTERED
BY BURGLARS!

The following poem, *The Dexter Tragedy*, was written by S.C.W. and first printed in an 1887 edition of *The Corinna Advertiser*. S.C.W., the Bard of Corinna, was Samuel Copp Worthen (1860–1940), who became a prominent Wall Street lawyer.

There was a time not long ago, Ere fashions had been altered so,
When grand and lofty themes alone Could wake the Muses sounding tone.
But now, since base ignoble themes, Can rouse the Poet's mighty dreams,
Since even Carmel's murdered tramp Can light the Poet's magic lamp,
With vain excuses I'll not tease, But just write down whate'er I please.
Some none or ten long years ago (The very date I do not know)
A fearful tragedy occurred, The like of which is seldom heard.
In Dexter's peaceful, thriving town, Where few dishonest men are found,
A man beloved throughout the land Fell 'neath a foul assassin's hand.
Some foolish or DESIGNING men—To say WHICH is not for my pen—
To prove have always vainly tried That 'twas a case of suicide.
But not a man of average brain, WITH NAUGHT TO LOSE AND NAUGHT TO GAIN,
Has ever for a moment thought That suicide was Barron's lot.
The murderers left no trace behind That anyone could ever find,
Except a certain greedy knave, Who was to cash a perfect slave,
And who would not his tale unfold, Unless his tongue was oiled with gold.
And since that time through listening Maine The question has been asked in vain,
Did local villain, tramp or crank Attempt to rob the Dexter bank?
But now, when years have rolled away, At last we see the breaking day
Which shoots its ray of truthful light Athwart the dark and crime-stained night.
At last the awful truth is known, The murderers' names at last are shown;
They are two rogues of cunning pith Named David Stain and Cromwell Smith,
Who now with faces stern and pale Are lying deep entombed in jail.
They lay and wait with fear and awe The dread machinery of the law,
Which works, as everyone must know, Not always sure though often slow.
But there is ONE who from above Will not forever shower love,
And even if they should in vain Try to convict the murderer Stain,
Then HE will deal with flaming rod The wrath of an avenging God.

Sam Perris (alias Worcester Sam) is still at large and wanted for the Dexter Savings Bank robbery and the J.W. Barron murder. Perris remains a prime suspect a century later, with a standing reward of $3,000 offered for his capture. He was a dapper French Canadian, largely respected in the bank robbing community, who was fluent in both French and English (which he spoke with no trace of an accent). He sported a scar on his face from a pistol shot on his right eyebrow, and alternately was whiskered or clean shaven. If you see Worcester Sam please report his whereabouts to the Dexter Historical Society.

James Hope (alias Old Man Hope), a friend and associate of Sam Perris, was also a suspect in the Barron murder. Jimmy didn't constrain his criminal bent just to the East Coast; he traveled to San Francisco, where he and some cronies attempted to rob the banking house Sauther & Company of $600,000. Hope was arrested, convicted, and sentenced to serve seven-and-a-half years at San Quinton. He apparently didn't like the accommodations and subsequently escaped.

Michael Kerrigan (alias Johnny Dobbs) was born and brought up in the slums of the fourth ward of New York City. He started his illustrious career as a pickpocket and later graduated to bank robber. Johnny was an associate of dapper Sam Perris, and was also a suspect in the Barron murder. He was accused of assisting Perris in throwing Barron into the vault after handcuffing, gagging, and choking the banker with the noose later found around his neck.

$1000 REWARD

On the 22d, instant,

DEXTER SAVINGS BANK WAS ENTERED

. Treas. Barron Murdered,

and an unsueccess fu attempt made to rob the safe.

Less than One Hundred Dollars Taken.

The Trustees of the bank do hereby offer a Reward of $1,000 for the detection of the Murderers, or any one of them.

A. F. Bradbury, President.

Four

The Age of
Economic Decline
1890–1899

"The flat," Dexter's Main Street as it appeared in 1892. Of special note is the large flag draped over Main Street, which was a common practice during political campaigns. At the top of the flag are the names Harrison and Reid: Benjamin Harrison was running for reelection as President on the Republican ticket, and Thomas Reid was the highly-respected Republican Speaker of the House in Congress. In 1892 Main Street was still unpaved and board sidewalks were in evidence. The Bank Block, the four-story building on the left side of Main Street, still had its mansard roof in 1892. A fire four years later burned the top stories of the building, and it was rebuilt to its present configuration. Also visible in the photograph are overhead electrical wires. By 1892 Dexter had electricity; for five years it was supplied by the Dexter Electric Light & Power Co., which generated the power from a waterwheel in the planing mill of the Eldridge Brothers shop on Grove Street.

A c. 1900 photograph of Gershom L. Gould's hay press and crew on lower Main Street. The hay press was run by two horses on a treadmill (at the rear of the press). Mr. Gould was an extensive purchaser and shipper of baled hay, shipping to points all across the east and south. He operated two modern hay presses that had a combined capacity of 20 to 25 tons per day. His storehouse, located on the Maine Central Railroad, had a capacity of 1,000 tons, and by 1904 he shipped out 4,000 tons of baled hay annually. In addition to the hay press business, Gershom also was a truckman, doing heavy trucking for companies such as Fay & Scott.

Dexter's railroad station in the upper village was built in 1889, when the railroad was extended from the lower village to Dover. Today, all that remains of this station is the metal sign on the canopy. A second nearly identical station without canopy was also built several miles north at Silver's Mills, also in Dexter. In this c. 1905–1915 photograph, an assortment of express wagons and hacks wait for the unloading of freight and passengers. With the coming of automobiles and better roads, passenger trains became a thing of the past, and the Maine Central Railroad eliminated passenger trains to Dexter in 1930. The railroad station was eventually purchased by Dennis Cleaves and moved up to Church Street, where it was fitted up into a grocery store. Dennis later sold the store, and it burned under the new management and was torn down.

Knight's store, Garland, Maine, in the late 1800s or early 1900s. This general store looks no different from thousands of others spread across the country. General stores offered a wide variety of merchandise, from graham and axe handles to candy, cloth, canned goods, and hardware supplies. In this photograph the proprietor is tallying up an order, while four men are gathered around the bulldog stove to settle the world's problems.

Willis W. Jackson loved horses. They say as a child he would crawl in the horse cribs to feed them apples and pet them. He spent most of his years on the farm now owned by his grandson, Alfred Lee, in Silver's Mills. He loved to drive fast and one evening, after attending a Grange meeting with his future wife, Lillian Pearl Grant, he proceeded to race home. This upset Pearl so that she refused to go with him, got out of the wagon, and went home with Ralph Jackson. Willis is shown here driving his father Charles Jackson's team around 1917.

Sam Ireland, Charles W. Curtis, John Hill, Dana Crockett, and son Ernest are shown here on a fishing trip to Moosehead Lake. All were Dexter business owners except Curtis, who was cashier, and then president, of the First National Bank of Dexter. He took yearly trips to Moosehead with varying companions. On an early trip as a "large boy" he went fishing while his companions went hunting. "I brought in sixty trout and we ate all for dinner."

56

Mary Ann Beals lived in the #10 District with her brother Ben "Bubby" Beals. She was a talented woman; besides doing all the household chores, she worked in the barn. She is shown here driving a team to town in her later years. Her brother Ben was a defining character in Dexter and was frequently seen walking Dexter's Main Street, always carrying a mysterious satchel that never left his side.

People for years wondered what was in that satchel. It had to be something special for Bubby to never let it leave his side. After he died the mystery was solved: it was his shoe lasts. It was said he could use it as a mold to make shoes for either foot. Erma Bentley believed that at some point a shoe cobbler who made Bubby's shoes probably told him these lasts were important, and to never let them out of his sight. Bubby's sister is shown here with one of the many braided rugs she sold around Dexter.

Bement Hill looking west toward Ripley from lower Main Street. The farm on the right at the top of the hill, purchased by Walter Bement in 1824 from Joshua Berry (the fiddler, as he was known), was called the Bement farm in the 1800s. The hill for many years was known for its rows of magnificent elm trees, planted in 1830 by Walter H.P. Bement, who dug the young trees up in the woods and transplanted them on the hill. During the summer of 1923, George Maxim (a former U.S. Army pilot and veteran of World War I) was in Dexter giving flying demonstrations and rides, using a field on Bement Hill to land and take off from. Kenneth Stafford remembered his first plane ride in Maxim's Curtis biplane: "The cockpits were all open to the air and there were no seatbelts. I was sixteen and was seated with "Tink" Parsons behind Mr. Maxim. "Tink" was older than I, probably in his mid-twenties, and as we took off I waved to the crowd on the ground and the slipstream caught my arm and wrenched it back. When we were in the air, "Tink" pulled out a bottle of bootleg liquor and we passed it around the plane, with each of us taking two or three swallows, including Captain Maxim. The ride lasted for ten minutes and cost each of us $10.00, a lot of money in those days."

The steamboat *Rita* at Waldheim Dock on Lake Wassookeag. It was built in 1882 by nineteen-year-old Arthur Abbott, grandson of Jeremiah, one of the Abbot Mill's founders. Arthur was a student at MIT and put his knowledge to use designing and building this 30-foot, 1,100-pound boat. He began his design in March. From April to May he worked every day cutting and fitting the ribs, planking, and caulking. The one-cylinder engine was bought, but he made even the rudder and tiller. On launch day *Rita* got up 20 pounds of steam in 30 minutes, and went 1/4 mile in 4 minutes with 60 pounds of steam.

Compliments of   **O. COPELAND,**

Ormandel Copeland ran his store, situated on Wall Street opposite the Exchange Hotel, from 1888 to 1906. The store contained a giant ice cream maker, which had to be turned by hand to make the ice cream.

A local newspaper advertisement for C.P. McCrillis, established in 1870. By 1908 it occupied two floors, each 2,400 square feet. Located on Church Street, the building is still in use as Dexter Motor Sales.

At the end of the century, young women following the wholesome Gibson Girl ideal became more athletic. Bicycling allowed them greater freedom even in clothing. The boater hats and full-sleeved shirts were often worn with full bloomers known as Turkish trousers, instead of skirts.

This cottage was built in 1888 by Frank Hayes at Waldheim. Waldheim, a summer colony begun in 1883 on the shores of Lake Wassookeag by nine Dexter men, is still in existence today. In its heyday there was a beach and boat dock, a bowling alley, a tennis court, a pavilion for dances and plays, and an ice house so the residents could make ice cream. The cottage shown here was later owned for thirty years by Harold Small, owner of the Grist Mill. It was next door to one his father and then sister owned. Several generations of children and their parents have had many wonderful summers in this "big happy family."

This photograph challenges modern readers to determine which side of Elmwood Cemetery that the driver, George Delano, was photographed on. Delano's delivery wagon from the Morse and Bridges Monument & Marble Works company stands in the foreground. The whitewashed farmhouse in the background stands in contrast to a huge gray boulder, which still sits proudly on the east side of the same farmhouse on Liberty Street today.

The Hi Wheeled Bike called the "Ordinary" was the rage in America from 1870 to 1890. First built in England, these bikes had 50 to 60-inch wheels with hard tires; they were more comfortable on rough terrain than smaller-wheeled bikes, but could never compete with the pneumatic tires that soon became common after 1890. Shown here are, from left to right: Dave Pomroy (who always dressed in style), John Dyer, Gus Pooler, and Adolph Pooler. Slim Prescott recalled the time as teenagers he and his brother Maynard took their family bike out of the shed to try it against orders from their dad. With Slim in an apple tree and Maynard steadying the bike, Slim jumped on and down the hill he went. It wasn't long before he did a "header" right over the front wheel and broke his nose.

Gus Pooler was the first "French kid" to graduate from Dexter High School. In those days it was common for the children of French descent to go immediately into the mills by age fifteen and never finish high school. Augustus Pooler was cut from a different cloth. Not only did he graduate, but went to work in a clothing store on Main Street and became well-respected in the business community.

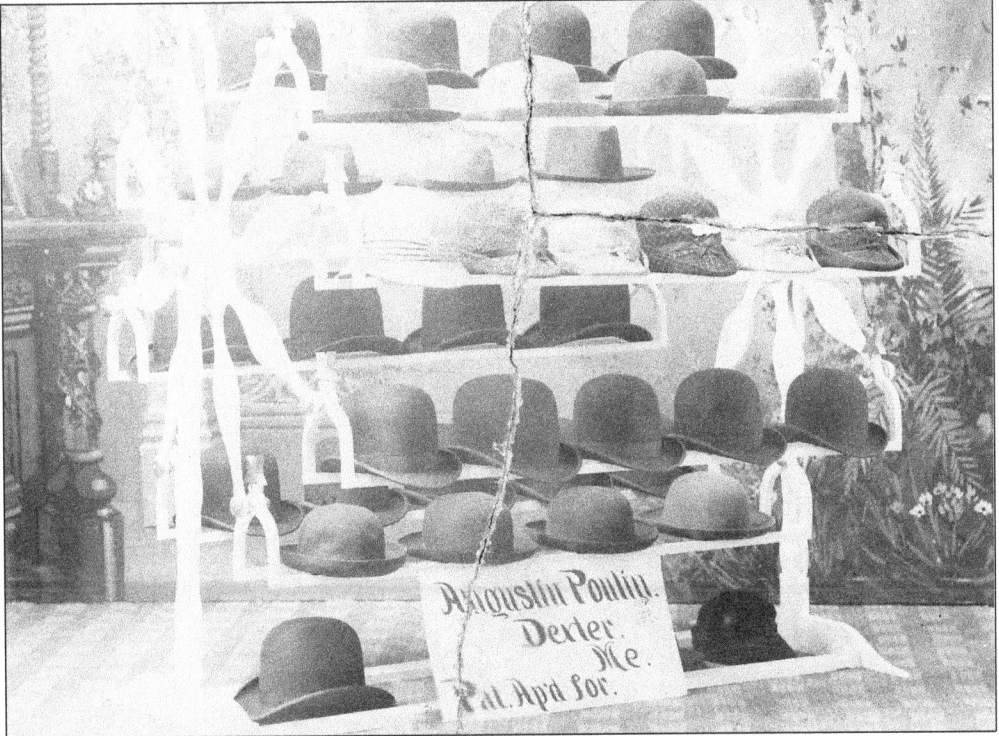

Working for N.W. Meigs clothier on Main Street proved a blessing for both Gus Pooler and Mr. Nelson Meigs. Gus's invention, a movable hat rack, was soon used in Meig's store and helped the business. Gus had it patented eventually.

Playing tennis was a favorite form of recreation then as now. This photograph was taken at the Pleasant Street Common, now the site of the local ice skating rink. Pictured here are, from left to right: Gus Pooler, Bert Call, Dr. Thatcher, and Charles Abbott.

The Dexter Boys Band, posing in the late 1800s for this photograph in front of the Universalist church.

A newspaper cartoon drawing and poem of Norman H. Fay, cofounder of the Fay & Scott machine shop and foundry. The cartoon depicts his many civic and business interests.

HON. NORMAN H. FAY OF DEXTER.

THE man who creates, from the crude idea, the machine that will do his will;
Who stands ready, at hand, to put into form, any device that was ever born;
And set it at work, in the aid of men, to battle the primal curse again;
To fashion the tool in its kindred parts, that, like the hand of man, will ply the arts
Or cause from the inventor's subtle brain, the dream of years to live again;—
Such men perforce, from their very selves, their missions large fulfil.

The man who receives, from his fellow-men, the reward that his works decree;
Who stands ready at hand as friend Fay has done, to serve to his best till the battle's done;
Who in business affairs or Board of Trade, or in legislative halls, has made
A record that fits to his record there, where the tool cuts true to the shade of a hair
And a life is lived that is full in line, with the Maker's drawing and design:—

In 1899 the Amos Abbott Company began the construction of a three-story brick addition to their mill on Church Street. The completed addition greatly facilitated the production of woolen cloth, and a 1917 Chamber of Commerce publication states that the mill had been producing over a half million yards of cloth for the past few years. The Abbott Mill was known for manufacturing heavy Mackinaw cloth of a very high quality, which became known as the "Abbott grays." This brick addition was later expanded twice in the twentieth century, doubling the length of the original brick structure.

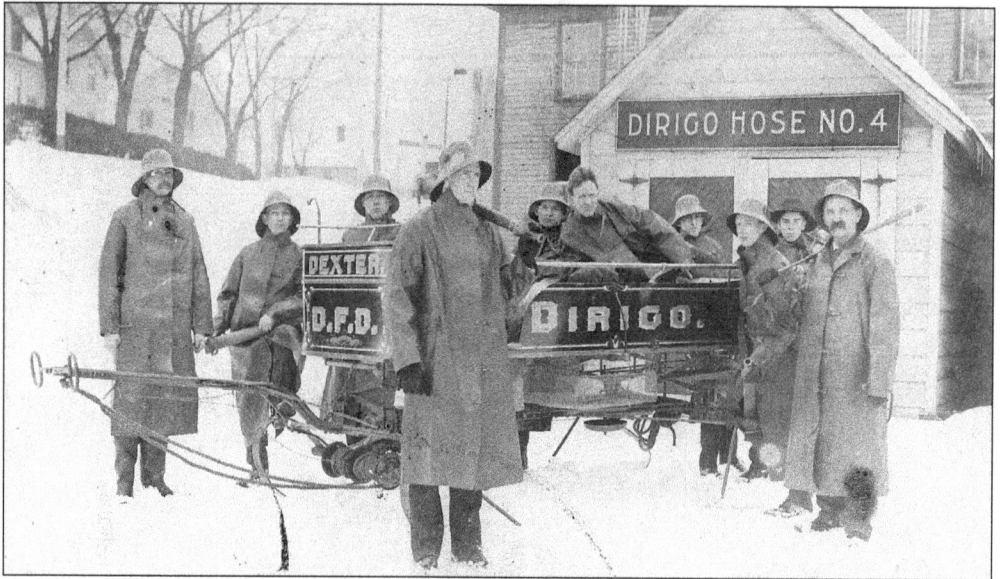

A c. 1890 photograph of Dirigo Hose Company No. 4 with their hose sleigh, taken near the Amos Abbott & Company dye house on Grove Street. From left to right are: Frank Shaw, George Hall, Frank Carne, Almont Grant, Harold Crosby, Willis Haseltine, William Jackson, Dr. Charles Ryan, Owen R. Brewster, and Charles Bean. Several members are worthy of mention: Owen R. Brewster went on to become governor of Maine, a member of the House of Representatives, and a U.S. senator; Harold Crosby became a composer of sorts, composing a number of military marches; Charles Ryan became a local veterinarian; Charles Bean was responsible for the building of several brick structures in town; Willis Haseltine was a businessman for many years in the harness business; and George Hall opened a canning factory.

It was 1899. The old Methodist church on lower Main Street would be torn down the following year. Bert Call went there once: he fell asleep at the service, his wife gave him hell, and he never went back. But here was his chance to make amends. This image, a time exposure made at night by the light of the moon from his attic window on Spring Street, was Bert's way of instilling a spiritual atmosphere in the photographs he took.

Henry Paine Dexter dedicated his life to building Dexter. He constructed up to eighty dwellings along with the Methodist, Congregational, and Catholic churches. He renovated the Universalist church. He built or renovated many of the business buildings on Main Street, including the present Ben Franklin, WGUY, and Jim Peakes Blocks. Mr. Dexter died in 1939 at the age of ninety-seven.

67

This steam-powered, 3-ton aircraft sported a 100-foot wing span. The craft was designed and built by Dexter resident Hiram Maxim, whose father conceived the idea in 1856. Hiram took sketches that his father had done and turned then into reality. Maxim's airplane flew in England in 1894, a full decade ahead of the Wright Brother's more famous flight at Kitty Hawk. Hiram Maxim, a native of Sangerville, was knighted by the queen of England for his accomplishments, which his native country was slow to appreciate and slower in accepting. Maxim's plane roared down 1,800 feet of railroad track balanced by out-riggers fitted on wooden rails. The craft was configured with two 18-foot propellers driven by steam engines that developed 362-hp, and it reached terrifying speeds, tearing up over 110 feet of rail as it slipped the bonds of earth and made history. Maxim and his three anxious assistants must have watched through ever widening eyes from their lofty perches in the open seating that could scarcely be called cockpits aboard the revolutionary aircraft.

Sir Hiram Maxim posing with his patented machine gun. Born in Sangerville, Maine, Hiram eventually patented over 270 inventions, and is credited with the car muffler, smokeless gun powder, and a self-closing mousetrap. He came by his inventive genius naturally, as his father had an inventive mind. In 1861, Hiram and Ed Fifield opened an agricultural manufactory in Middlesex District making corn shellers, winnowers, etc. He stayed only a year before moving on to greater fame with his machine gun.

In 1890, he came back to Dexter to test fire his machine gun on the shore of Lake Wassookeag near the present float bridge. Many in town were surprised at how easy the gun fired. Hiram had the naive hope that his invention would end war. In the above photograph he is demonstrating his gun to foreign dignitaries after it sheared off a large tree. Hiram eventually sold the patent rights to the German Army, who used the water-cooled machine gun against the Allies during World War I.

This photograph shows the Call Studio, as it was known, on Main Street. Bert and his crew sold gifts, jewelry, and hand-colored black and white photographs until he retired after being on Main Street since 1887. He took portraits of the majority of people within twenty miles of Dexter. This is presently the Dexter Cafe.

By 1924 the Call Studio had a reputation for being one of the most up-to-date photo studios in New England. The props Bert Call had on hand to use with his fine studio portraits were a marvel to behold. As his reputation spread, many people that came to town requested tours of the studio. They were never refused.

70

" 'I was in my twenties when I met Bert and I learned a lot of Dexter history listening to him; he was a natural story teller. You could say he had a kind of serenity about him, too. His life was marked by personal tragedy but his attitude was: It's God's way and I'm going to live with it. He had a wisdom and strength I admired.' Frank Spizuoco believes that Bert Call never realized the value of his own work. The picture that emerges from the tapes, from the remarkable photographs, and from the recollections of the people who knew him is of a man who was part poet, part philosopher, and not much concerned about commerce and the accumulation of wealth. 'He never sent bills to his customers. They'll pay when they can, he'd say. Perhaps that kind of serenity helped him focus on his art.' "

Frank Spizuoco, as quoted by
Richard Sprague for an article in
Maine Line (Fall 1988)

The top photograph is a fine print made by Bert Call at his studio on Main Street. The bottom photograph is of Foss Pond around 1890. From left to right are: Wint Fay, Fred Herrick, Ervin Call, and Bert Call. This was one of the favorite camping spots of Bert Call, his family, and his friends.

Through the civic interest of George A. Abbott, the Dexter Town Library became the property of all town citizens on Christmas day, 1894, for the token sum of $1. The dollar is a gold coin that was passed on from Mr. Abbott to the next generation of Abbott family members and remains as a tradition to this day. To say that Mr. Abbott was far sighted and generous would be a gross understatement, as he not only purchased the property on which the library was built but personally funded the magnificent building that stands prominently atop a knoll at the intersection of Main, Church, and Pleasant Streets today.

Five

The Dawn of a New Age 1900–1919

A washout on Zion's Hill looking east onto Main Street, taken sometime between 1896 and 1904. Zion's Hill, also known as Dustin Hill, received its name from a hill in Kennebunk, Maine. An article from the July 12, 1906 edition of the *Bangor Daily Commercial* tells how Zion's Hill got its name: "According to Mr. Foss, Elder Nathan L. Thompson moved here prior to 1842 from Kennebunk, Maine, and built himself a residence, the house now occupied by Charles R. Favor on Zion's Hill. When a resident of Kennebunk, Elder Thompson was a resident of Zion's Hill in that town, which is really the chief residential section and he therefore christened the hill here after that in Kennebunk."

Whether in a conversation or at the annual Town Meeting, Ed Chase was sure to bring up "Christ and Democracy" sometime before he was finished speaking.

A VISION.

DEXTER, MAINE, MARCH 16, 1903.

Last week I visited the beautiful village of Waterville, the place of my birth, 61 years ago in a few days. As I viewed the wonderful developments that have been performed by the labor of man I was struck with amazement, and I said to myself as I scanned it over: "This is grand! This is a picture that no artist can paint; it took the power of God." Then I thought of my father and mother, and remembered how they had toiled that I might be what I ought to be, a man. And I thought that if my philosophy of life be true, they were beholding the beautiful scenery before them with a greater vividness than myself. And the scenery grew grander as I contemplated.

If selfishness could be replanted with true love what a happy place this earth would be. But selfishness and love cannot exist together in great abundance.

As I strolled about I met a friend and he said: "Ed, why don't you come down and make this your home. We would like to have you. Your brother is well fixed." I told him I had a little diamond in Dexter that was handsome and pure now as an angel, and I wanted to be where she was to protect her from selfishness, so that she might grow up and make others happy, as she does now.

I thought of Christ, and Washington, and Paine, and Lincoln, and a host of others, and remembered some of their good deeds and felt that I ought to do like them so far as I could to show my gratitude.

Another beautiful picture I saw on a Sabbath morning about eight o'clock when the sun was shining bright. The sidewalks seemed full in all directions with people coming home from Mass, where they had been to worship God. I said to myself: "Is not this grand, to behold so many who have toiled all the week, resting."

And as the vision passed I beheld what appeared to me many faces and all with happy countenances, as much as to say: "Your vision is true," and among them were my father and my mother.

E. H. CHASE.

A pen on paper sketch of the White Mill on the corner of Mill and Water Streets, done by Roland Gilbert, a long-time resident of Dexter known for his artistic ability. The sketch was done in 1940 and was completed before the spectacular fire that engulfed the mill in July of that year. Ed Chase, whose family was actively involved in this mill until it burned, was one of Dexter's most interesting characters. He wrote several short stories, including one wonderfully insightful vignette entitled *The Vision*, that reflected his impressions about Waterville, Maine, and the love in his life whom he'd left behind in Dexter. There is one particularly colorful story about Ed, a train, and a litter of pigs that bears repeating. It seems that Mr. Chase was the engineer on the train that ran between Newport and Dexter. His farm was located near the tracks, and when his run was done he would use the train to pull stumps and move slop. One day, while tending a litter of hungry pigs at the farm, Ed realized that the engine had worked up a head of steam on its own and left the farm behind, chugging off down the track to Corinna. In a panic Ed legged it back to the telegraph office in Dexter, wired Corinna, and pled his case in a hurry to Corinna agent Herbert H. Fisher. Fisher responded in a timely fashion by ordering his section crew at the car house to hurry over to "Reverse Curve," about a mile north of the Corinna station. Arriving on a hand car in the nick of time, the men scrambled aboard the errant locomotive, saving the day along with Chase's hide and job.

An advertisement for John F. Bigelow's livery and carriage business, taken from a *c.* 1880s Exchange Hotel register. John F. Bigelow was a long-time and well-known dealer in carriages and sleighs until the automobile pushed him out of business. He was born in 1850 in St. Albans, Maine, and came to Dexter in 1879.

The Mandolin Club, *c.* 1903. This was one of the many musical groups that played and performed in Dexter at the turn of the century. Without television and movies, the favorite social outlet in the community was live theatrical plays or musical performances. Pictured here are, from left to right: (first row) Louise Bridgham, Imogene Bumps, Charles Dustin, and Angie Ryan; (middle row) Willis Haines, Clara Hayden, Ralph Bridge, Clyde Pingree, and Charles Brewster; (back row) Carl Morse, H.N. Gardner, Mary Hatch, Ethelinde Bridgham, Bertha Leighton, Fay Kinney, and Ralph O. Brewster.

76

A sunny Sunday afternoon in 1910 found the local aristocracy motoring off to Lakewood to enjoy the day's latest playwrights and plays. Pictured here are Wint Fay, Will Brewster, Bert Call, and Norman H. Fay, along with their families.

It happened on the morning of February 8, 1905. The morning mail train No. 82 from Foxcroft was heading south through Dexter. Mary Hatch Howard was looking out the window from her home as she so often did when the train went by: "As I looked I saw the engine become wobbly, and finally fall over. I knew it was a cold day and the few passengers came into my house to get warm. There was a milk car and the milk was spilled and running. The building shown is where the hearse was kept for the nearby cemetery." The accident split and uprooted a large maple tree. Mr. Peakes, the engineer, suffered a dislocated shoulder. The cause of the accident was that an iron beam forming the framework broke in two and the cowcatcher dropped onto the tracks.

The executive department of the Fay & Scott machine shop and foundry. From left to right are: Norman H. Fay, Winthrop "Wint" Fay, unknown, and Myrtie Leighton. Florence Leighton recalls two cats she took care of in 1943. She was working for the town, when invited to work at Fay & Scott with Myrtie Leighton in Peter Plouff's office: "(They) found two kittens and named them Fay and Scott. The employees took care of them in the office, where the kittens lived in a box and had the run of the place. After about a year, they let the cats out into the shop to chase mice. The cats loved to be out in the shop and rode back and forth on the planers."

A c. 1900s photograph of the Fay & Scott shop, with its veritable jungle of belts. At this time the shop was probably still extensively water-powered. Tim Hill is on the far left, with Lynn Jewett at the machine, and Benny Jones on the far right. The Fay & Scott shop was founded in 1881 by Norman H. Fay and Walter Scott. In 1884 a new plant and foundry was constructed on the site of the former Copeland Woolen Mill, which had burned in 1868. The company's initial products were wood-turning lathes used to make peavey handles. Eventually, the shop expanded into engine (metal) lathes and a wide variety of contracted machines for American industry. A Fay & Scott lathe was on the battleship *Maine* when it sank in Havana Harbor. The Navy sent the lathe back to Fay & Scott to be reconditioned when it was salvaged from the wreck. Fay & Scott went on to produce a large amount of war ordinance for the U.S. military during World Wars I and II.

Pouring metal at the Fay & Scott foundry in the early 1900s. This photograph was obviously staged for the photographer, as rarely would three pours be done simultaneously. The foundry was built in 1884, and it changed little before it was razed in 1972. It was a valuable addition to the Fay & Scott machine shop, and allowed the factory to reproduce nearly any metal part required. Foundry work was one of the dirtiest and hottest jobs to be found in Dexter. Florence Leighton, a secretary at the plant, remembered the foundry well: "There were piles of sand inside the foundry for use in making the molds, and at dinner time the workers would grab their lunches and sit down anywhere to eat." Florence always hated to go to the foundry at lunch because "the men fed the rats that burrowed up from the sandpiles to beg for food." The rats always knew when it was mealtime! Workers were allowed to make cast-iron frying pans, doorstops, banks, and bootjacks on their lunch hours. One condition of this privilege was that the men could only use cast iron in making their offhand pieces. The only marked piece known is a sitting cat doorstop marked Fay & Scott.

A Dunbarton weave room in 1919. These spoolers and dressers, from left to right, are: Reginald Gilbert, Lucy Groleau Anaire, Mabel Cyr, Phil Clukey, Millie Trundy, and John Clukey. A woolen mill was first built on this site in 1836. After a fire it was rebuilt in 1844 with stone quarried from Witherell's Island, which today is owned by Dennis Cleaves. The Panic of 1857 wiped out all ownership of the woolen mills in Dexter and they went into receivership. In 1898 the Stone Mill, as it was called, was sold to the Penobscot Woolen Company, which was composed of a group of Dexter citizens. In the early 1950s, Paul Barstow purchased the mill and renamed it Crown Alexander. It closed in 1970 and was torn down in 1974. The last twenty years the mill had manufactured primarily automobile fabric.

This distinguished looking officer is Dexter policeman Forrest Johnson. Forrest posed for this picture complete with fashionable waxed mustache in 1915. He was the father of lifelong Garland resident Frank Johnson.

Hattie Whitten was placed under house arrest only after her second daughter was found poisoned. She found a way to elude her accusers, however, when a local sheriff's wife, Mrs. Curtis, brought her two requested towels from her satchel in the hall. Leaving Hattie by herself for a moment too long, the sheriff's wife reentered the room to find Mrs. Whitten hung from her bed post by her neck, allowing the reputed murderess to escape her own remorse as well as any court's conviction.

Jennie Whitten   Hattie E. Whitten   Fannie B. Whitten

Three-year-old Jere Abbott, steering his father's boat on Lake Wassookeag, around 1906. After graduating from Bowdoin and Harvard, Jere was asked by his former Harvard roommate Alfred Barr to assist him in founding the Museum of Modern Art in New York.

"Jere had spent 1923 and 1924 in Paris where he met Gertrude Stein. A sensitive gourmet and a talented pianist with a lively sense of humor, he had delighted in regaling Barr's Wellesley students with stirring dissonant renditions of works by Stravinsky and Les Sic."

Alice Goldfarb Marquis, from *Missionary for the Modern* (1989)

While horse-drawn sleds were a familiar sight at the turn of the century, this impressive load of cargo was reputed to be the single largest express load for one client at one time from the American Express Company. It was delivered from Etta Hewey's Millinary Shop, across from the Abbott Memorial library on Church Street.

Will exhibit at DEXTER, TUESDAY, JUNE 24.

P.T. BARNUM'S ILLUSTRATED NEWS

Copyright by P. T. BARNUM, 1879.   The Courier Company Show Printing House, Buffalo, N. Y.   The Largest in the World; Fire-proof.

A page from the June 1879 edition of P.T. Barnum's *Illustrated News*. This very early "promotional paper" is profusely illustrated and displays most of the major performers and acts associated with the circus. An advance team had arrived in Dexter a month earlier, probably to scout out the site and arrange promotional materials, etc. The circus was an annual time of excitement in Dexter; with its parade and pageantry, it gave the town an exotic air, which was just what socially starved and mostly isolated farming families, mill workers, and children needed. One story regarding the circus that has been passed down involves the floating bridge across the "narrows" of the lake before 1860. The bridge tended to move and sway and the inclined ramps at each end were so heavy that water several inches deep covered the top of the bridge. This tended to spook some animals not used to the situation. Tradition states that one circus coming to Dexter decided not to take its animals, especially the elephants, across, for fear that they might panic and do harm to themselves and the bridge. Instead of crossing, the circus took the long way around the lake through Ripley.

A circus elephant and camel parading up Park Street, on the way to the circus grounds located on Beech Street, on July 15, 1909. The earliest circus site on record is the "town lot" or "common" located between Church and Pleasant Streets (now the site of the town's ice skating rink). The lot was donated to the town prior to 1842 by Jonathan Farrar, and it was used for circuses, menageries, etc., until the Pleasant Street School was built in 1886. The circus grounds were then moved up the hill to Beech Street until the construction of Judge Arthur Stone's home in the early 1900s. Crosby Park has also been used in the past to house circuses.

Circus elephants cooling themselves at the fountain in Crosby Park during the 1920s. This park was created in 1906 with the substantial help of Oliver and Simon P. Crosby of St. Paul, Minnesota, former residents of Dexter. The park was created out of a grove owned by Virgil Crockett, and its original dimensions were 17 rods wide by 26 rods long. The pavilion in the park was constructed in 1913, and in 1931 the present grandstand was constructed by the American Legion for their baseball league.

Alvin A. Eastman's fruit farm, c. 1910–1915. This farm, located on land between Pleasant and Prospect Streets, covered an area of about 5 acres. In 1911, it produced 300 bushels of currants and gooseberries, 30 bushels of raspberries, and 125 bushels of plums. In a 1912 *Lewiston Journal* article Mr. Eastman stated: "When I took this place 32 years ago, it was wild land. I cleared the forest and began with the Downing gooseberry which I consider the best variety . . . The raspberry is also a good fruit and much easier to cultivate than the strawberry. I have found the business profitable and one to which our farmers should give more attention. Personally I market my crop in Boston, but with the rapidly growing army of summer guests, our own state will furnish all the market needed in the future."

The Gossip Club of 1915 having a good time talking or maybe gossiping? We'll leave it up to the reader to decide what these ladies are saying. From left to right are: (front row) Kay Smart Page, Anne Couire, and Estelle "Aunt Teddy" Hill; (back row) Elsie Hill Sharpe, Marguerite Brown Cloutier, and Mary Coughlin.

86

"February 23, 1907. Dexter has a $70,000 fire. Fierce conflagration Friday night fought with difficulty. With the temperature at 15 degrees below zero and a stiff breeze blowing, the most destructive fire in the history of the town visited Dexter Friday night and was still burning at a late hour Saturday. Seven stores were damaged, two tenements gutted, and several offices damaged. As soon as the fire was discovered the occupants were aroused and all had narrow escapes, owing to the dense smoke and rapidly spreading flames. The wind blew a stiff breeze and things looked dark for the business section of town. The whole fire department, assisted by scores of citizens, soon had five streams of water playing on the building. The water kept up its force well and the pumps were kept working getting water from the reservoir. Had it not been for the new water system the whole business section would have been totally destroyed. The firemen suffered intensely from the freezing water and the intense cold. They soon appeared like animated ice cakes but were often treated to hot coffee and sandwiches by the Exchange Hotel and the Dexter Club where a ball had been going on at the time the fire started. So far as can be determined, the fire was caused by a defective chimney in the building owned by Charles F. Witherell."

from the February 23, 1907 edition of the *Eastern Gazette*

Anyone who was around Dexter as a child in the early twentieth century will remember the Jose farm (on the corner of Liberty and Spring Streets) and Jose's Circus. Later on Bennie's Diner took over the corner and today a Mobil station is located there, but in the early days the area was all farmland. The circus was held for neighborhood children on the hill in back of the old N.H. Fay High School. The Jose family was an artistic, intellectual family with a love for education and music, and the legacy they left lasted for many years. Their children were Sybilla, Carlton, and Lewis. Doug Pooler became friends with Sybilla toward the later end of her life and was called on to help clean out the home when Carlton died. To his amazement he discovered a library on the second floor complete with stacks like a public library. Carlton's extensive collection of art books was donated to Abbott Memorial Library. There was also a lab where Carlton had been cutting stone and was making jewelry rings. Carlton had a machine shop in the shed and after working second shift at Fay and Scott he would work there at home. During World War II he developed a unique technique for making ammunition for the war effort and sold this to the government privately at a large profit. He also made furniture and Doug recalled a self-portrait on the wall in his library. Lewis was a spinner at the Amos Abbott Mill for many years. Before he died he was busy learning Chinese. Sybilla worked for Wentworth Laundry and at one point in her life became a "mail order bride" in West Virginia. But it didn't work out, so she returned to Dexter and resumed her family name.

Hallie Jose sitting in front of his home with his favorite pet. He was a farmer and always had a yard full of animals along Spring Street. Hallie Jose married Mildred Covel, but died early in life from pneumonia after spending time in a cold rain getting in the cattle from the pasture. He is long remembered for Jose's Circus, which was a yearly event for local children between 1912 and 1915 (see p. 88).

Mildred and Hallie Jose dressed in their fine attire after a musical evening entertaining. Mildred was a very soft-spoken person and the musical entertainment she provided was always for family and a small circle of close friends. In the evenings she and Hallie entertained themselves with Abbie Nutter at the piano.

Dexter's water sprinkler, c. 1915, used to keep the dust down. The cost was 25¢ per house. This is Andrew W. Keyte's team of horses with Mr. Shorey driving. Dust was a yearly problem during the late summer months, until paved roads became more common.

A horse-drawn school conveyance at the Spring Street School in 1920. Some of these early wooden "school buses" even had a stove to keep the children warm.

Dexter's Main Street, known as "the flat," as it appeared in 1901 all decked out for the centennial celebration of Dexter's settlement. The parade held on August 14, 1901, had over sixty interesting units including: a team loaded with noisy boys labeled "Products of Dexter"; one hundred girls dressed in white on a large elaborately-trimmed float, each representing a year in Dexter; the Standard Oil cart with its pretty trim; Ervin Farrar's milk cart; and the three "locomobiles" owned by S.S. Ireland, Norman H. Fay, and Dr. Thomas J. Springall. Main Street and all public buildings were extensively decorated with bunting, and the town hall carried a large circular picture of Admiral Dewey and a picture of the battleship *Maine*. The celebration was kicked off on the August 13 with a band concert on the flat and a large bonfire on Bryant's Hill. At sunrise the following day all the bells in town were rung and one hundred guns were fired on Bryant's Hill. Festivities continued throughout the day as Dexter had its largest celebration since 1876.

91

The old Dexter House sitting in the middle of "the flat," before it was moved down lower Main Street to its eventual resting place across from the Methodist church, c. 1906.

Moving the old Dexter House, c. 1906, to make way for the new Morrison Memorial building, now the Dexter municipal offices. This was the second time the building was moved; in 1876 it was moved from the lot directly above. The building was moved down lower Main Street and set across from the Methodist church, where it became a tenement building.

A Christmas parade on "the flat" sometime between 1896 and 1906.

The graduating class of Dexter High in 1904, before the use of caps and gowns. From left to right are: (front row) Effie Bailey, Annie Dresser, Alice Young, and Ida Littlefield. (middle row) Jessie Roberts Mower, Elizabeth Losle, Annie C. Ward, Ethel Carsley Fortier, and Lucy Gordon; (back row) Grace Hutchins, Freeman Sands, Bertha Warman, Duane Mower, Hattie Atuates, Harold Crosby, and Edna Carr.

The whole school had about eighty students and four teachers. It was housed in a building on Spring Street which was later used as an elementary school. Three courses of study were offered: College, Classical, and English. Football was taken seriously and basketball was just beginning to be played. There was a new orchestra as well as older banjo and mandolin groups. The *Signet* was the student publication. It contained exhortations to fellow students to be less rowdy, to stop littering the halls, and not to smoke on downtown street corners, as well as literary pieces and the usual student jokes and alumni news.

The Frank Sampson family ready for a Sunday drive, c. 1908. From left to right are: Frank Sampson (1867–1909), Mary Sampson Salisbury (1899), Harold Sampson (1894–1968), Ken Sampson (1906), and Laura Sampson (1870–1936). Clarence Sampson, who supplied this photograph, was born about three months after this picture was taken.

A "welcome home" dinner on Main Street for Dexter's returning World War I veterans, June 12, 1919. Two hundred and seventy-seven men from Dexter fought in the "Great War"; ten died while in the service. Many of the men fought as part of Dexter's National Guard unit, Company A, which was one of the first American units to land in France under General John "Blackjack" Pershing. On its return, Company A members smuggled back a captured German Maxim machine gun, now housed at the Dexter Historical Society's Grist Mill Museum.

The following poem by Ralph Waldo Emerson, called *Hamatreya* (1847), characterizes farmers of Concord, Massachusetts, their preoccupation with their land, and where it got them:

Bulkeley, Hunt, Willard, Hosmer, Meriam, Flint,
Possessed the land which rendered to their toil,
Hay, corn, roots, hemp, flax, apples, wool and wood.
Each of these landlords walked amidst his farm,
Saying, "'Tis mine, my children's and my name's.
How sweet the west wind sounds in my own trees!
How graceful climb those shadows on my hill!
I fancy these pure waters and the flags
Know me, as does my dog: we sympathize;
And, I affirm, my actions smack of the soil."
Where are these men? Asleep beneath their grounds:
And strangers, fond as they, their furrows plough.
Earth laughs in flowers, to see her boastful boys
Earth-proud, proud of the earth which is not theirs;
Who steer the plough, but cannot steer their feet
Clear of the grave.
They added ridge to valley, brook to pond,
And sighed for all that bounded their domain;
"This suits me for a pasture; that's my park;
We must have clay, lime, gravel, granite-ledge,
And misty lowland, where to go for peat.
The land is well, lies fairly to the south.
'Tis good when you have crossed the sea and back,
To find the sitfast acres where you left them."
Ah! the hot owner sees not Death, who adds
Him to his land, a lump of mould the more.
Hear what the Earth says:
Earth-Song
"Mine and yours; Mine, not yours. Earth endures; Stars abide- Shine down in the old sea;
Old are the shores; But where are old men? I who have seen much,
Such have I never seen. "The lawyer's deed Ran sure, In tail, To them, and to their heirs
Who shall succeed, Without fail, Forevermore. "Here is the land, Shaggy with wood,
With its old valley, Mound and flood. But the heritors?- Fled like the flood's foam.
The lawyer, and the laws, And the kingdom, Clean swept herefrom.
"They called me theirs, Who so controlled me; Yet everyone Wished to stay, and is gone,
How am I theirs, If they cannot hold me, But I hold them?"
When I heard the Earth-Song
I was no longer brave;
My avarice cooled
Like lust in the chill of the grave.

This 1918 photograph depicts a common sight in Maine even as recently as twenty-five years ago. A.W. Keyte's teams is shown on Abbott Hill, the present site of Dexter's primary and secondary schools. Quincy Smith is "building load" behind the team of Bill and Harry in 1918. At this time, changes were beginning to happen in agriculture that are still going on today. The course of change in Maine has mirrored national trends. In 1880, Maine had 3.5 million acres, over 33% of the land, cleared for farming; today only 600,000 acres, less than 5%, is open cropland. Between 1860 and 1890, 5,000 farms were abandoned, mostly on poorer soils that should never have been cleared in the first place. The U.S. population at this time was growing fourteen times faster than Maine's. It wasn't until 1960 that Maine reversed the 100-year trend of rural areas losing population to the larger towns and cities. This new rural influx kept up from 1960 until the 1980s, when it finally subsided.

Charles Favor, an accomplished practical joker, ran a harness shop in Dexter. In 1888 he and dentist Dr. C.H. Haines renamed and revived the Oriental Dramatic Company, which began performing plays on Christmas 1868. The new group, Favor and Haines Dramatic Company, had many years of success even after both partners' deaths in 1922. Erma Bently directed many of the later productions into the 1940s. Dr. Haines played banjo and Favor, with a faulty memory, sometimes had to improvise. Fortunately, his lines were often superior to those forgotten. They also wrote their own skits and songs that reflected community events.

Wint Fay (of the Fay & Scott Manufacturing Co.) and a compatriot in one of Favor and Haines plays, which were really community productions involving many townsfolk both on stage and behind the scenes. Although "amateurs," they produced professional results, including the sets, which once featured a stream of real running water. Usually done at the town hall, the shows often traveled to other towns as well.

Six

The Roaring '20s and the Depression Age 1920–1939

Dexter's Main Street, "the flat," as it appeared between 1925 and 1931, looking west from the intersection in the center of town. In the foreground granite cobblestones are visible, installed in the early twentieth century to facilitate travel through the intersection. The stones were laid beginning just below Grove Street and extended through the intersection to the point where Spring Street enters Main Street. They are still there today underneath the asphalt.

The first railroad station and platform at Silver's Mills as it appeared in 1889. Later a standard Maine Central railroad station was constructed in the same spot and remained until it was torn down in the late 1940s. In the foreground is the bridge over Main Stream; to the middle right a small portion of the sawmill property can be seen.

A c. 1920 hunting trip involving Ridge Road residents. These deer were shot at a camp in Shirley. The photograph was taken in front of Will Nichol's residence and barn by Puffers Pond, where Horace and Perry McKenney currently milk cows. From left to right are: Cell Crowell, Jim Ballard, Elwin Puffer, Winfield Frost, Alton Puffer, Ross Mason, and Willis Nichols.

100

Ernest Dennison Blaisdell came to Dexter in 1905 and was an early pioneer in the automobile business in central Maine. He was a kindly boss and had frequent parties for his crew and the salesmen from his different businesses. This photograph was taken was during Prohibition, but Ernest always seemed to have plenty of liquor around. Orman Gerry recalled one party at a camp on Crawford's Island, where everyone was knocked out by the strong bootleg booze before 10 pm. Another amusing incident happened when Elbridge Atwater lost a Presidential election bet and had to wheel Harry Brawn down Main Street in a wheelbarrow. The event drew a good crowd along the way.

The Universalist church, located on Church Street and built in 1829. This building was the first church structure to be constructed in Dexter. During the 1820s some citizens wanted the church built in east Dexter nearer to the Garland line, but others favored building the church at "the mills." Jonathan Farrar finally decided the issue by offering a plot of land at "the mills" for a new church.

A photograph of Idella Robinson Mower and her ten pupils at the North Dexter School in 1925. From left to right are: Doris Ellingwood, Inez Hall, Dana Luce, Minnie Amazeen, Gladys Hall, Idella Mower, Eugene Hall, Thomas Ellingwood, Wilfred Colbry, Robert Elderkin, and Walter Elderkin. The one-room schoolhouse would soon become an endangered species in Dexter. As roads became better and transportation more efficient it made sense to close the outlying rural schools and incorporate the students into the village schools to save money. The school committee already had a policy of not opening rural schools unless there were at least eight pupils per term. This building still stands and is the home of Ken and Nancy Beckwith in North Dexter.

"Nancy The Clock." This what John L. Morrison had inscribed on a slate sign attached to the clock tower he had built in memory of his wife Nancy in 1925. The clock was built by the E. Howard Clock Company for an estimated $850. Harry Young and Arthur Page are shown here on top of the clock. The clock stopped sometime in the 1970s, and not much was done about it until a curious Doug Pooler inquired about it. He remembered hearing it in his early days and wondered why it had stopped. He was promptly handed the key, went up to the tower, pushed the pendulum, and it started. By default Doug has become Dexter's "keeper of the time." It has been running regularly since 1980 and Doug does regular maintenance, repairs, and sets the time as needed. The clock runs by electricity to wind and lift the weights automatically. It is the only one in the area to do so. The lights are on a timer. Some years ago, "Shirley and his bunch of yahoos got to drinking up there and did some damage," Doug said. It stopped for awhile until Dana Wilbur got it going and has been running ever since.

Georgia Titus (1862–1938) grew up with her aunt and uncle on a farm in West Garland near the Dexter line. She learned to sew and memorize verse and enjoyed her one-room schoolhouse days. Her attempts at attending Dexter High School and teaching in rural schools were thwarted by her ill health. Although she had to live quietly at home she expressed her love of beauty through needlework, painting, and poetry. Many poems appeared in local and state papers, and a book, *Rose Jar of Verse*, was published after her death.

The following is one of her poems, entitled *The Village of Dexter*:

God held it awhile in His own right hand
Then gave it a place in the heart of Maine;
Cradled it there in the hills of sand,
And nurtured it with the summer rain.
Covered the valley with winter snows,
Cushioned its chalice and gemmed its edge
Or dropped down a wreath of the wild June rose
To drape a crevice, or hide a ledge.
We who recall it tonight, behold
It memory a slope between
Low hanging curtains of sunset gold,
With a cross etched in a band of green;
And higher yet than the white homes creep,
Where the bluebirds fan the air,
See harbored in clouds its port of sleep,
For the scar of its graves is there.
And what if the days are a little late,
The gay dawn scatters the lilies' bloom
On the deep blue mirror of the lake
Whose seepage turns the busy loom.
And what if its sunsets are premature,
The hands of the toiler weave and spin,
And the ties of friendship are strong and sure
In this vale of sunshine that God shut in.
The heaven smiles with starry eyes
Above long winding snow-wreathed aisles,
Where hurried footsteps in their beat
Press down the drift to pave a street;
Across each way some glimmering home-light streams
Flooding the darkness with a shaft that gleams
Like silver, in a river, winding low
In shadowy glades where mosses grow.

105

When French-Canadians first migrated to the U.S., they faced the same suspicions, prejudices, and ill treatment that strangers usually faced in a new community. In the early 1920s a Klavern of Ku Klux Klansmen paraded their white-robed bigotry in Dexter for a span of about three years, while focusing their hatred primarily on the Catholic residents of the area. The local "Klavern" membership included many otherwise respectable citizens, and may have even boasted a future governor of Maine, who was elected with the money and support of the Klansmen. The Klan's activities included several large parades and a cross burning on the top of Bryant Hill in the Catholic portion of Mount Pleasant Cemetery.

Charles Bean and his crew at the Spring Street School, building the chimney for the Manual Training shop. The year is about 1924. Mr. Bean is on the scaffold, with "Greasy" Goulette and Bennie Champeon mixing the mortar.

Jim Stonier's glory days as Dexter's football coach wouldn't be complete without mentioning this 1930 team. It was said that Omar Cloutier (#4) could outrun a deer (rumor has it that he did race against an Essex Motor car). Bill Conway recalled that their favorite football play was to eject a teammate from the huddle and send him off the field. They would line up, start the play, and then throw the ball to this player, who by this time had slipped past the line of scrimmage unobserved along the sideline, and was downfield to receive the pass for a touchdown.

Jim Stonier's reputation carries on today. A stern disciplinarian, he is still warmly remembered by his former students. Jim started in Dexter in 1916 and at one time turned down a chance to play on Jim Thorpe's first pro football team in the U.S. "Tough Jim Stonier had a soft heart, a heart bigger than a basketball," said a Hatch Prep 1950 brochure. Jim is standing in this photograph with the cup; his wife is to the right.

107

The Page boys of Dexter after a successful fox hunt. The hunting was done on Horn Hill at the head of the pond and the boys were accompanied by their father and George Leighton. The boys are the children of Almon and Kathryn Page from lower Main Street. Sam (left) is holding "Trim," Jake has the 410 shotgun under his arm, and Almon Jr. is proudly holding the foxes. This photograph was taken in front of George Leighton's home on Cedar Street in 1932. Note the Essex Sedan in the background.

A 1933 view looking south on Spring Street in front of the present Rite Aid drug store. On the right is the fire hall and Bailey Motors. This new concrete road used 25,000 bags of cement, according to Preston Richardson, who claimed to unload every bag when it arrived in town.

Sightseers at the construction site of the new post office. After being shifted up and down Main Street for one hundred years, the post office finally got a place of its own around 1939.

A 1928 advertising gimmick. The first twenty-five new Maytag washing machines arrived in Dexter at Bill Ayer's store (now Ben Franklin). Wonder how many residents actually brought their dirty clothes to wash in public?

Sam Fellows (left) gives a trim to Jim Boynton, while Bob Roberts works on Tom Smart. Sam's shop was located on the second floor of the Fish Block (Tillson True Value). A sign inside the door of the shop read: "This isn't a battery shop, so don't say charge it!"

Herb Downing's moose hanging in front of the Dexter Livery Stables, c. 1930. This was reputed to be the last legal moose (or the first illegal moose) to be shot as the law was changed to prohibit moose hunting in Maine. The moose head was stuffed and hung for many years in Downing's garage on Grove Street.

The waterslide at the "Birches," Dexter's summertime hot spot during the 1930s. For a nominal fee you could ride a flutterboard with casters down the incline and skim across the water. The area also sported a beach, float, and refreshments.

Homer Gordon standing in front of his radio sound car, which was a familiar sight to Dexter residents for many years. Homer provided sound at many town events, as well as advertising for businesses and events, while he drove the sound car through town.

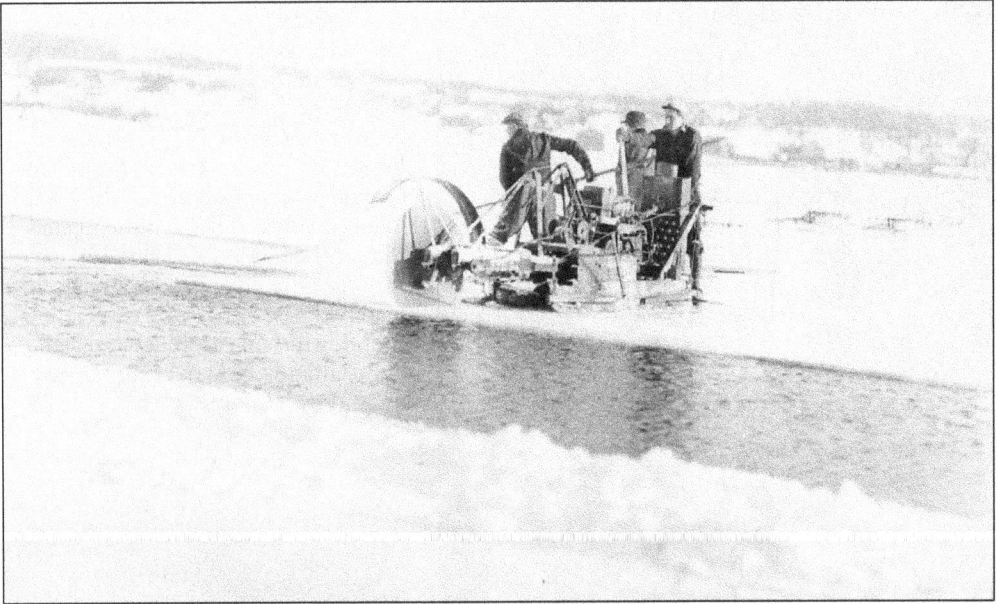

Cutting ice on Lake Wassookeag was modernized in the 1930s when Homer Wilbur got involved. He took an old Franklin car and rigged up a plow on both ends to plow off the snow. For an ice cutter he rigged up a model T engine hooked to a differential and had a 58-inch circular saw mounted on it. He could set it to cut ice of any depth and had a PTO to pull itself forward or backward. Ernie Robinson is show here running the saw.

Dexter's toboggan slide on Abbott Hill about 1940. The slide emptied out onto the big lake (Wassookeag) and offered riders a big thrill. Kip Landry remembers sneaking up to the slide the night before it was scheduled to open with three friends from school. A bright full moon illuminated the site as they took off down the chute. What the four did not plan on was running through the large puddle of slush and water at the bottom. The slide did not stay up very long because the town officials worried that young boys riding their bicycles down the chute into the lake might get hurt.

"Joe Baker's army." Joe was a local boy with the NYA (National Youth Administration) at Fay & Scott during the Depression. He was coordinator at the NYA and was known for his expertise as a baseball coach. As a captain he ran the local National Guard. It was remembered that as the National Guard was leaving Dexter for World War II, they marched past Fay & Scott; everyone shut down their machines and came out to the roadside to cheer our boys on as they left for war.

Joe Baker's army spent many an hour shooting on Hersey Hill. This photograph was taken in 1935, and shows the National Guard at rifle practice there. Today the area is a wooded forest, but the large concrete wall where the targets were placed and the six mounds down the hill where the boys shot from still exist.

114

Back along, when anyone thought of the state of Maine, they often thought of potatoes. Dexter has had its share of potato farms, as can be seen in the above photograph. But today Maine is something else. Susan Trausch, in *The Boston Globe* in 1992, portrays the new Maine through the eyes of "those from away." She writes: "The fantasy is Maine. Living there. Getting away from here, wherever here is. Leaving it all behind. Quitting a good job and buying a farm. Or an inn. Small town. No expressway. No commute. The simple life. Nice folks. They come for the quality-of-life stuff of cleaner environment, beauty, and the advantages of small town living. The dream lives and maybe it's not so crazy, or maybe a lot of people are nuts. Terry and Mark Silber purchased Hedgehog Hill farm as a weekend retreat. Gradually it took over their lives. Terry left her art director's job at *Atlantic Magazine* and Mark turned his back on tenure at Boston University. In the city one spends so much time on politics and the presentation of self, Terry says. One cannot talk without being clever. Life here is much less self-conscious, more sensual. I'm not pressed to perform here. Life is a process not a product."

"I came to love my rows, my beans, though so many more than I wanted. They attached me to the earth, and so I got strength like Antaeus. Removing the weeds, putting fresh soil about the bean stems, and encouraging this weed which I had sown making the yellow soil express its summer thought in bean leaves and blossoms rather than in wormwood and piper and millet grass, making the earth say beans instead of grass,—this was my daily work. I was determined to know beans. When they were growing, I used to hoe from five o'clock in the morning till noon, and then commonly spent the rest of the day about other affairs. But labor of the hands, even when pursued to the verge of drudgery, is perhaps never the worst form of idleness. It has a constant and imperishable moral, and to the scholar it yields a classic result. Ancient poetry and mythology suggest, at least that husbandry was once a sacred art; but is pursued with irreverent haste and heedlessness by us, our object being to have large farms and large crops merely."

Henry David Thoreau, from *The Bean-Field in Walden*

The E.D. Blaisdell automobile dealership on Grove Street in 1909. The Blaisdell garage was the second auto repair garage to open in Dexter, the first being at the Fay & Scott factory (1906). In 1909 the Blaisdell dealership was selling Maxwell, Ford, Buick, and Overland cars. In 1911 the company built a spacious dealership on Spring Street and by the 1920s it became one of the leading auto dealerships in central Maine with a branch in Skowhegan. The company suffered a severe fire in 1925, but rebuilt.

The Park Theater as it appeared during the 1920s, with Marvin Salisbury standing in front of the marquee. The theater was built in 1912 by Dr. Charles H. Haines and Charles H. Wyman and opened on July 3, 1912. During the 1920s stars such as Gloria Swanson and Rudolph Valentino dominated the silent screen, but by the mid-1920s the new "talkies," or sound films, were revolutionizing the business. The theater operated until 1968 and was irreparably damaged in a roof collapse during a snowstorm in 1969.

Ever viewing life through the eyes of an artist, Bert Call captured an almost perfect photograph when he took this shot. The huge piece of drift wood as a central image, but Indian Pond—with St. Albans in the background, and a bevy of local bathing beauties—adds to the symmetry and esthetics of this classic black and white photograph.

Seven

The Age of Peril and Prosperity 1940–1959

Dexter's Main Street as it appeared in the 1940s and 1950s. On a Friday or Saturday night Main Street was the place to be in Dexter. Restaurants and stores remained open late, and the theater and bowling alley provided amusement—but some people liked to just walk down the street to visit and socialize with friends. You had to get there early for a choice parking place.

Dr. H. Edward Whalen, shown here welcoming Dr. Hans Sherman to town, practiced in the Dexter area for over twenty-five years until his death on March 3, 1948. "Doc" Whalen was a well-known and beloved member of the community; no distance was too far for him to go, nor was it ever too late to answer a call. In addition, he was a familiar figure and a constant inspiration to the men who frequented Tommy's Station (a group that came to be known as "Club International"). So moved was this group at the loss of "Doc" that Reverend Gordon Reardon felt compelled to put into print a permanent tribute to him from the "gang at Tommy's" (see p.121).

"DeDa" (on right) was what stuck, although her given name was Floreda Dyer. Her nickname came from an older sister, but her fame came from what she did: in December 1948 she won the State of Maine Bowling Championship, and, up to that time, only one person held the title longer than she did. Many Dexter residents will remember Deda from her days working at the A&P and later Bud's supermarket.

The following was the tribute paid to "Doc" Whalen by Reverend Gordon Reardon and the "gang at Tommy's": " 'The International Club' of Dexter, Maine, an organization without charter, by-laws, memberships, dues or visible assets, extends to the wife of our friend, his daughter, and his sons, and to his more distant relatives, our deepest sympathy in a loss which transcends our immediate realization. He was an inspiration to this group which included priests and preachers, poets and pedagogues, merchants and laborers—men of all races, creeds, classes, and conditions of life who, in the informality of the rocking chairs to be found in the spacious window of a filling station, found the important things of life which we call democracy. Here, free speech was the rule and not the exception; here minorities gained prestige; here, the foibles and shortcomings of all present were subjected to good natured open diagnosis; here a sense of decency and a sense of humor were the sole requirements for admission . . . Here, honest opinion was demanded; here, no man's family prestige, educational advantages, or economic security provided him with an advantage over his fellows . . . It was in this place that his kindness, his generosity, and the warmth of his personality gave vent to the bigness of his heart. Men with big hearts wear them out early in the service of others. This he did for a quarter of a century in this community until the great heart of a good Catholic, a good father, a good physician, a good citizen, and a good friend ceased to beat at the age of fifty. The little white house across from the club with the shingle reading H. Edward Whalen, M.D., Physician and Surgeon, is dark this night. The lights have also gone out in the hearts of his fellows, who sit in silence and gaze at the little building where men and women and children were made whole and restored to health. But the Eternal Light still burns in the hearts and minds of those who loved him, and the memory of his good life will be cherished unto the Perfect Day."

An aerial view of Dexter's business center, taken in 1939–40. The new post office (center left, next to the First Baptist Church) had just been completed. The Dunbarton Woolen Mill can be seen in the upper left, and the Abbott Memorial Library, town hall, and Universalist church appear in the right foreground.

This photograph shows "specking" at a local woolen mill, one of the last processes to find flaws in the material before going to the sewing room. Martha (the "weave room drop wire-girl") Titus spent twenty-two years at the Amos Abbott Company. "I loved to go to work, so many wonderful people," she fondly recalled recently. She also discussed the different processes and recalled some of the workers. The picker house had Blaine Williams, with Marvin Williams as boss of the card room. The wool continued to the dye room, spinning room, and then the spool room. Next was Mat McNair and Arthur Bailey, dressers. The weave room bosses through the years were Ralph Richards, Bob Mayo, Tom Ambrose, Clatus Clukey, Dutch Lancaster, and Linwood Easler. Ida McNair and Cora Cogan were the drawing-in girls in the weave room. Loom fixers included Bob Goulette, Roland Atwater, and Bobby Smith. Next was Pat Poulin, percher. Betty Clukey was in the sewing room. Specking in the sewing room were Jean Dudley and Bea Farnum.

One of Dexter's more colorful and warmly-remembered clergymen was Father Cornelius Enright, a long-time parish priest who demonstrated what "Working for our Lord" meant to him—a phrase he was well known for. Although of Irish descent (as most of the parish priests throughout central Maine were), Father Enright appreciated and respected the rich French heritage of his flock and read the Sunday gospel in French as well as English. From time to time Father Enright could be found in the Sterling or the Gables sitting with the "common" people playing cribbage or planning a trip to the horse races with members and prospective members of his flock. Some of his horse-racing companions readers may recognize include: Lloyd H. Hatch Jr., Raymond "Lefty" Ronco, George Green, Fernald Goulette, and long-time local barber Charlie Trembley. On one occasion Father Enright was visiting the Gables when a member of a smoke-damaged Methodist church solicited him for a contribution to help rebuild the church. Reaching for his wallet he remarked that, while he wasn't able to donate money to help build a rival church, he could donate money toward having the damaged walls torn down, which he did. Mention his name to Protestant or Catholic alike and their faces light up with warmth and remembrance of Father Enright, who embraced and embodied the word "ecumenical" long before his beloved church hierarchy did.

124

The presentation of the Minuteman flag at the Army/Navy E award ceremony at Fay & Scott, on July 29, 1944. Fay & Scott was an important part of New England's war production effort during World War II. Over six hundred men and women worked in the factory and the E award pin they received was a very select award, being given to only 3% of all munitions workers across the country. During the war, Fay & Scott made a variety of war ordinance including bullet-stamping machines, rifle-propelled grenades, radar units, and hand grenades. Fay & Scott still functions today, but with about one tenth of the workers it had during World War II.

The wedding breakfast of George Ramsdell and Marie Ronco at the Sterling Hotel in 1949. From left to right are: George Ramsdell, Marie Ronco Ramsdell, Elsie Beaupre Ronco, Laddie Wintle, Warren "Washy" Ronco, Father Enright, Marilyn Ramsdell Wintle, unknown, Victoria Michaud, Alice Ronco, Newton Ramsdell, and Anna Ramsdell Martin.

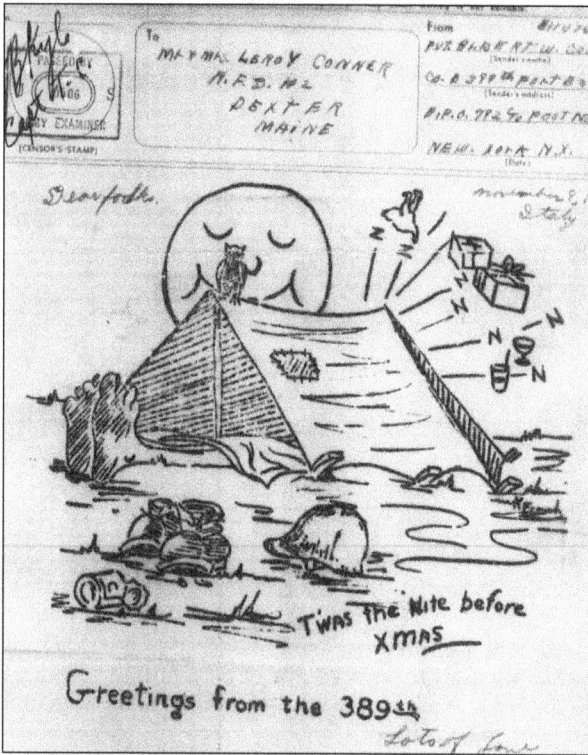

World War II was a frightening time for our country. This photograph is a Christmas card from Weldon Connor to his folks in 1943 from the 389th in Italy. Dexter fully supported the war effort, with over five hundred of its citizens joining the military. Gerald Gilbert, Armand Poirier, Arthur Bailey, and Ralph Tetu were POWs. Russ Titus was in the Philippines when the bomb hit Japan. Martha Titus was shocked when his letters were cut up by the censors, so when Russ came home on leave they devised a code to trick the censors so she would know where he was when he wrote to her. Ray Whitney mentioned in his letters how beautiful the flack was from the pilot seat of his bomber out of Italy. Dexter lost twenty-four servicemen during World War II.

The Fay & Scott Victory Band posing for a group photograph in front of the factory office at the time of the Army/Navy E award in 1944. From left to right are: Earl Pomroy, unknown, Olie Larson, Arthur Haseltine, Bobby O'Connor, Rex Slater, unknown, Bob Cinqmars, Lawrence Ronco, Nellie Haseltine Brasier, Anna Crouse, Rita Clark, unknown, Joyce Page, unknown, unknown, Bob Tillson, Elbridge Atwater, Clyde Merrill, Fred Haseltine, Tim Haseltine, unknown, Harold Hatch, and Carl Crawford.

Fred Quigley's Manual Training class at the building adjacent to the Spring Street School. Pictured here are, from left to right: Stan Wark, unknown, Leon Hammond, unknown, unknown, and Roger Mountain.

Jack Roberts was Dexter's premier farmer. He took a run-down farm and with determination and tenacity developed fertile soil and a fine herd of Jersey cows (see p. 135.) He started Robert's Dairy and sold bottled milk in town for years. He also was in the legislature in Augusta, representing this area's interests.

Fossa's store as it appeared for Dexter's 150th celebration in 1951. This store was a fixture on Dexter's Main Street for over fifty years. It was started by Mario B. Fossa, who came to Dexter in 1924 from Milo, where he had run a fruit and confectionary business. He first was located on lower Main Street, but soon purchased the remains of James Kerby's store and built the two-level store pictured here, which was patterned after a similar building he had seen in Chicago. Mario retired from the business in 1950 and his son James took over the business. The building burned in the fire of 1978.

The Amos Abbott Company Woolen Mill as it appeared probably during the 1940s. The woolen business was already in its final days in Dexter during the 1940s. Changing demands, styles, competition, and environmental concerns helped to bring about the demise of the woolen industry in Dexter. In 1975 the Abbott Mill decided to close their doors after 155 years of ownership. Today the site is owned by Guilford Industries and is used as a warehouse.

128

The Eldridge Brothers chimney on Middlesex Avenue was a landmark. Directly across the Main Street from the Call Studio (now Dexter cafe), Bert must have viewed it often before he decided to photograph it. The print was enlarged and hand-colored, like many that Bert and his studio crew did. The first coloring of pictures was done on tin-types, with a bit of red powder being touched on the cheeks before the type was varnished. In 1915 Bert began to color pictures, landscapes only, and two or three years later he began to use water colors to color the photographs. By 1930 oils had taken their place.

Hockey practice at the Hatch Preparatory School on High Street. Lloyd Hatch began the school in 1926; known then as the Wassookeag School Camp, it pioneered the concept of combining excellent scholastics with fine athletic programs. This boys-only boarding school attracted students from across the country and even around the world.

Don Colbath (1899–1960) touched many lives. As the local ice man he knew everyone in town. He was a hard worker with great strength, but his great heart is what he is remembered for. "He could give to another so much of himself." And everyone remembers "Joe," Don's pet crow. The crow was seen all about town except on the milk delivery days, when he was locked up. Seems he had the bad habit of taking the caps off milk bottles as they were delivered to neighbor's homes.

This is the ice house by the Float Bridge on the shores of Lake Wassookeag. Dexter has had its share of colorful ice delivery men. George Brawn, at the turn of the century, is remembered on his ice wagon with the tools clanking as he growled "giddap," always three times, to move his team along. Don Colbath bought the ice business from the Hudson Ice Company in 1943 and ran it until refrigerators were plentiful. Then he sold the Coolerator brand. Don would fill the barn shown here with ice every winter, using up to twenty men to help him. He loved people, had a mischievous sense of humor, and loved to act up in a crowd. Often Don would invite people home for a meal. Erma, his wife, expected it and was always prepared. Don delivered ice to many poor families, even when not paid. After Don died, over $3,000 in unpaid bills were found in his desk. His is remembered by his children as "A common man in appearance but an extraordinary man in strength of spirit and generosity." I guess that's the measure of a person's real success; the way your kids describe you.

Bert L. Call and his bear. The following quote best describes Bert Call's life in Dexter: "I wish so to live ever as to derive my satisfactions and inspirations from the commonest events, everyday phenomena, so that what my senses hourly perceive, my daily walk, the conversation of my neighbors, may inspire me, and I may dream of no heaven but that which lies about me."

Henry David Thoreau, from his journal entry of March 11, 1856

A tragic short ride and near miss. On May 21, 1941, twenty-three-year-old pilot Gerald Brewster, nephew of Senator Ralph Brewster, decided to treat Joseph Mountain Jr., James Michaud, and Shirley King to a ride, while logging some more miles toward his commercial license. The hydroplane took off at 11 am from the Grove Street side of Lake Wassookeag and ascended 75 feet, heading inland, before the motor stalled. Brewster tried to turn back toward the lake but didn't make it. The crash in the driveway of the Nichol's house on Church Street was followed immediately by an explosion and sheet of flame. Brewster crawled out unaided, while townspeople helped Mountain and Michaud. All were bruised and burnt. King, tangled in wires with his head on the burning motor, was the last extricated. All were rushed to Plummer Hospital, accompanied by Dr. Whalen, and then taken to Bangor, where King died that evening. Joseph Mountain Jr. also died from his injuries.

132

The governor gets a haircut, just like a regular guy. Ralph Owen Brewster, son of a Dexter grocer, was a teacher, lawyer, governor of Maine, and a U.S. Senator. His home on Zion's Hill is now the Brewster Inn, a bed and breakfast. George McIntyre's barber shop was on Main Street in what is now the Judkins Insurance Agency. His wife Linda had a beauty salon in the back.

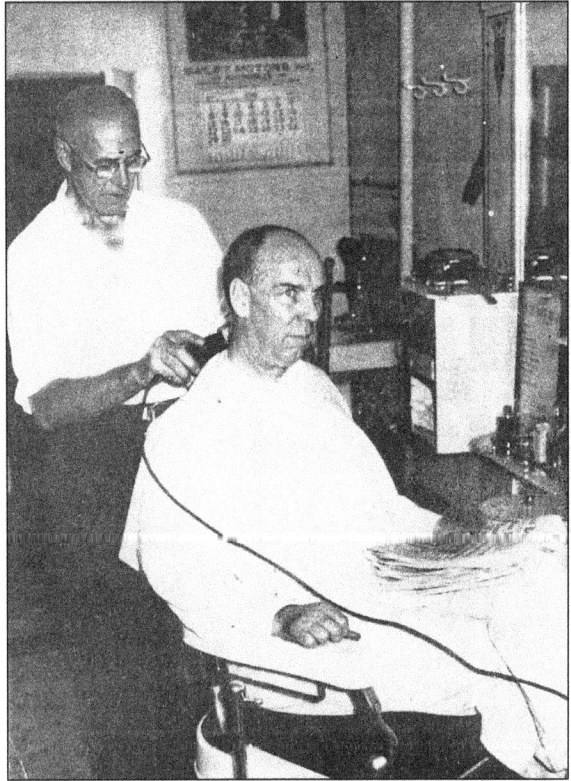

The "End Men" are shown here in black faces at a Dexter's Minstrel Show of the 1940s. These shows were patterned after Van Armann's traveling minstrel shows that were common for the time. Dexter's show was put on by various social groups in town to raise money. Louise Gudroe usually ran it; she was a good organizer and she knew music.

Frank Tait, born April 7, 1854, was long a familiar sight in Dexter as he lived to be nearly one hundred. He worked many years at the Abbott Mill. Renowned as a fisherman, he spent many hours on Lake Wassookeag. He said he once saw something at least 20 to 30 feet long with several humps on its back moving speedily to the surface for about 5 minutes before disappearing. Our own Lock Ness monster?

In later years Frank lived with farmer Arthur Fish on Garland Road and then on the corner of Free and Main Streets. No matter where he was he would go in the predawn hours to wake his buddy Jim Leighton (who lived in the former Greene Tavern) to go fishing.

Frank P. McKenney was born in Newport and was a farmer all his life in Dexter and Corinna, producing beans, potatoes, and milk. But he is probably best remembered for what he stored in his shed for a few days. Doing a favor for a hired boy, he unknowingly harbored the body of a Mr. Corson, who was murdered at the Green Gables Bar (Eight Tenement) on Water Street by the hired boy's father, Gene Knight. The trunk with the body was hauled off to Athens, but the FBI eventually recovered it, and Mr. Knight was arrested and put into prison.

This was a familiar scene on every country road in Dexter up until 1960. A small dairy, with a herd of ten to twenty Jerseys, Holsteins, or Guernseys providing a modest income from working on the land. This herd is from Robert's Dairy at the corner of Silver's Mills and Dover-Foxcroft Roads.

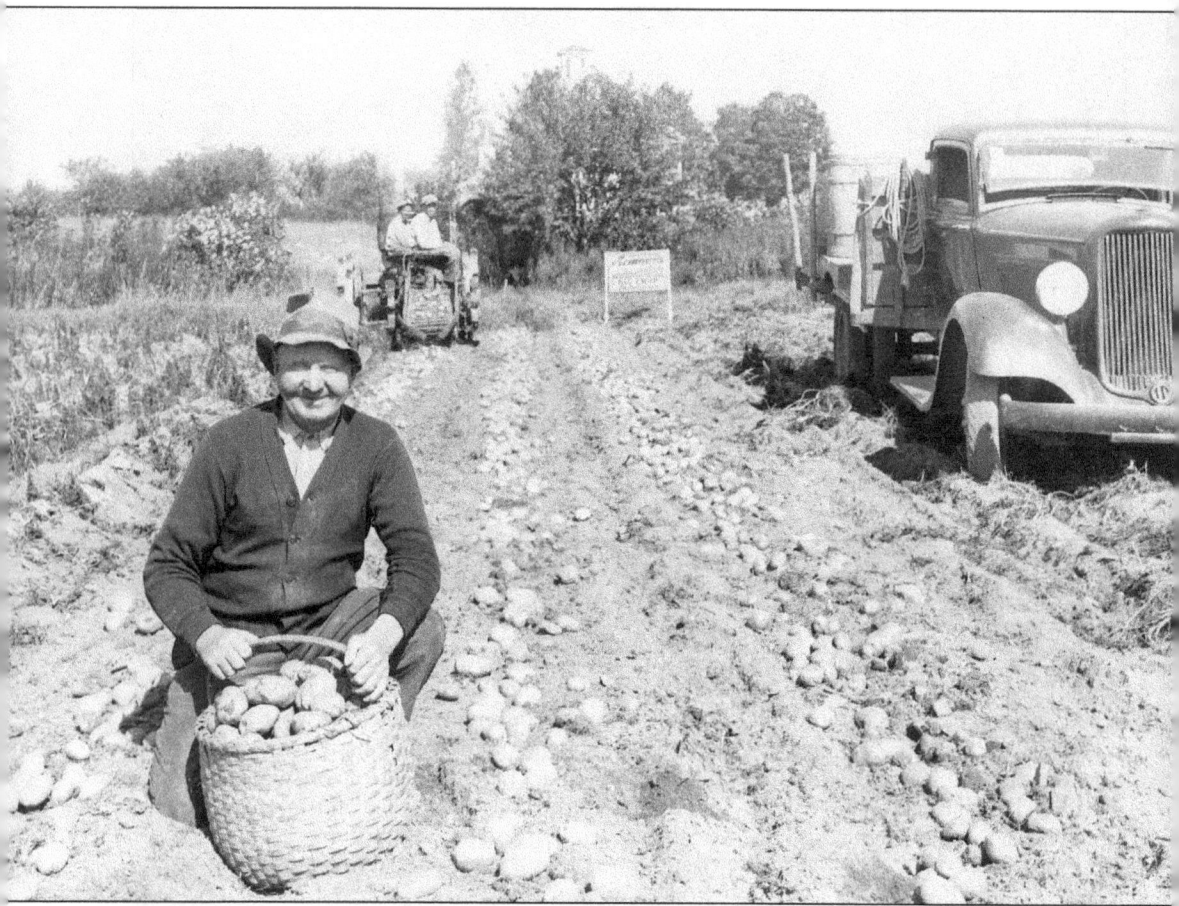

This photograph is one of many that Bert Call took of the countryside in the 1930s for the Armour Fertilizer Company. It's obvious this man is proud of his accomplishments; it was a labor of love to produce such an abundant potato crop. A typical wage paid to a picker at this time was 10¢ a barrel.

"The aim of the laborer should be, not to get his living, to get a good job, but to perform well a certain work. Do not hire a man who does your work for money, but him who does it for love of it."

Henry David Thoreau, from *Life Without Principle*

Will Arsenault's haying crew in North Dexter on July 18, 1945. On the load, from left to right, are: Will, Anne Robinson Bennett, Richard Robinson, John Blanchard, Marie Blanchard, and Francis Blanchard. Uncle Alfred Arsenault and Ernie Robinson are on the ground.

Hanaford and Carrie Crouse farmed on Ripley Road for over forty-two years. Hamp was a large rugged man with gentle ways, except during haying season. Then he would tear around to insure getting his crop in the barn in a timely manner. He always hired six or more of the local boys to help. This was a favorite place for haying due to the famous cooking and baking of Carrie. Then, after haying all day, Hamp would treat the boys by taking them to the "Birches" for a swim.

Dexter had its share of blacksmiths through the years, but none more colorful than Pat Fields. Pat ran a shop in town for many years, and would head up into the North Wood for the winter to take care of horses at the logging camps. This photograph shows Pat at newly-opened Camp Dexter on Lake Wassookeag in 1956.

Clyde Willard was a farmer all his life on Cambridge Road by Main Stream. As a young man he worked in lumber camps up north. One day he was asked to lead a stubborn horse past the cook shack, where the horse was known to always balk and refuse to move. Everyone in camp was watching the "kid" and ready to laugh. When the horse stopped, Clyde pulled and pulled to no avail. He then walked into the cook shack and came out with a very hot potato. He lifted up the horse's tail and placed the hot potato in the appropriate place. Needless to say, the horse promptly moved and never pulled that trick again.

This is Benny Robinson's pulling team from Dover-Foxcroft. Benny worked for "Blind" Al Tracy in Garland, and as was the custom, would work the horses all week in the woods and go to horse pulling contests on the weekend. This photograph is possibly below Ted Clark's house on the Shore Road. Joe Downing had lived on this farm before Ted bought it. He was famous locally for his hard cider and many a person would trek up from the lake after ice fishing or skating to get a jug to bring back to the bonfire. Seems Joe got caught one winter in Bangor selling cider during Prohibition and was locked up for a while. After serving his sentence, when it got time for his release, he refused to leave. He stayed all winter despite Sheriff Orman Fernandez pleading with him to leave. Dexter was billed $5 per month to cover the costs until the spring, when Joe left and came home.

From summer camp owner to football coach, from superintendent of schools to harness horse breeder and trainer, Don Holsapple has had a varied existence in Dexter. His first accomplishment was being instrumental in forming the LTC Football League in central Maine, which Dexter then promptly dominated for many years. He is fondly remembered accepting the Coach of the Year Award from the *Bangor Daily Commercial* but thanking the *Bangor Daily News* at the ceremony. For a good story, ask him about the time the horses at Camp Dexter broke out of the pasture and ended up in Les Reese's corral. Before the melee ended the sheriff and the state police were involved. Don is shown here on Good Luck; on the other ponies, from left to right, are: Ritchie Koplan, Larry Graham, and George Musig.

Red Buttons, *c.* 1959, was a favorite with children because of their ice cream and soda. It originally stood at the Esso station (Exxon today) when Vern Bodwell and William Russell purchased it. One Sunday, when people passed by, they realized it had disappeared. Vern decided to move it to the public beach, and got Bud Ellms to do the job. Bud put it on two logs and dragged it through the streets early Sunday morning. They just took it and went without saying a word to anyone. It has since been renovated many times. Later owners were Phil Mealey, Mackie Wilbur with Charlie Crawford, Ron Haley, and recently Peter Prescott and Joanne Hibbard. It is now known as Lakeside Lunch.

Eight

The Modern Age
1960–1996

Dexter's Main Street as it appeared one night during the Christmas season in the late 1960s. This is a time exposure, which explains the mysterious-looking trails of light. Note the star, the wreaths, and the christmas lights: Main Street is dressed up for the season, and you can almost feel the spirit of Christmas in the air.

Dexter has never been the same since George Campbell came to town. An energetic town manager, he is shown here with the head of the CETA, a national organization that put people to work doing useful civic projects, and Wes Sherburne (left), chairman of the town council. They are standing in the newly-renovated parking lot where the old grist mill pond had recently been filled in. George is showing the result of a grant he obtained that revitalized the areas around the Grist Mill Museum and the former Dunbarton Mill further downstream along Water Street. George liked to tell the story that at one time the town council said to him, "George, no more new projects. You're going too fast for us, slow down."

A symbol of both change and continuity: the Brick Mill became Dexter Shoe but remained a major employer for the Dexter area. Built in 1848 on the corner of Water and Liberty Streets by Foss & Conant as a woolen mill, it was enlarged several times and also changed owners from Farrar & Cutler to Dexter Mills to Wassookeag to George Park Mfg. Regardless of its official name, it was always known as the Brick Mill.

In 1957 forty-three-year-old Harold Alfond bought the Brick Mill and began Dexter Shoe. Alfond went to high school in Swampscott, Massachusetts, and then worked in shoe factories in Derry and Newmarket, N.H., and Kennebunk, M.E. In 1940 he and his father began Norrwock Shoe Co. in Norridgewock. Alfond is well-known in Maine as a benefactor to many college athletic programs and other organizations to benefit children.

This was a familiar scene in the lower end of Dexter, as Fred Staples and his mare Peg head home after spreading cow dressing on someone's garden. Sometimes, when Fred imbibed too much, he would lay down in the wagon and Peg would weave through the streets of Dexter to get him safely home. Don Brown made the mistake of offering a cigar to Fred once when he first came to his store to buy his weekly groceries. From then on, Fred expected a cigar, and got one every week until he died.

144

Many in Dexter remember Fred and Peg. He never refused a child a ride. Three-year-old Jill Goulette is shown here with Fred on his "dressing" wagon. Fred impressed Sue Goulette so much that she sat down and wrote the following poem as a tribute to Fred and Peg. After Fred died, and before he was buried as instructed in his will, a large hole was dug by Bud Ellms with an incline leading down to the bottom. Hay was put in the hole and Peg was led down the incline. Dr. Watson then gave the horse a shot to put her to sleep and she was covered up. Fred's funeral was then held.

Fred and Peggy
The rubber tires roll soundlessly
Under the familiar wooden wagon
A giant black mare clip clops gently along
Under the loving reins of her
Constant companion and doting admirer
The smell of leather harness
Of horse
Of cherry tobacco
The Santa Claus smile
Caress the senses of the children that gather
"Can we pet Peggy, Fred?"
"Can we give Peggy a carrot, Fred?"
"Hey Fred, can we ride up the street with you?"
Watching the tar roll away
Under the sun
And under our happily swinging feet.

"A good man who did a good job." Chief of Police Harold Knox was known as an exacting enforcer, but he was evenhanded and played no favorites. A long-standing rumor has recently been clarified by his wife Donna. Harold did ride a horse into the movie theatre entrance, on a dare from Harvey Hatch, while Judy Plouff was buying a ticket. But he did not ride it into the theatre and down the aisle toward the screen, as had been gossiped for years. Harold is shown here with Major John Hyson in front of his convertible, one of many he had through the years.

Always ready to lend a helping hand, Lucian Dube willingly consented to his son Ted and friends storing a barrel of cider in his cellar over the winter. Lucian is shown here on Mothers' Day, 1961, helping bottle the fermented cider. Needless to say, Charlene and Lucian's mothers were not too happy about spending Mothers' Day washing out two hundred quart bottles. Their displeasure was heightened even more when Lucian couldn't walk up the stairs after he was done.

The year 1976 marked the nation's bicentennial; it was also the 160th anniversary of the signing of Dexter's town charter. On June 17 at the Grist Mill Museum there was a reenactment of this event. Some of the original signers were represented by four costumed residents who are their descendants: Katherine Pinkerton (from Edward Jumper), Ruth Dudley (from Ebenezer Small, the first settler), Robert Buxton (from Benjamin Jennings), and Dorothy Briggs (from Isaiah Lincoln).

Roger T. Gilbert (on left with President L.B. Johnson) was Dexter's "Man of the Year" in the 1950s. He learned the value of hard work and discipline from growing up on a farm, and worked diligently to ensure the quality of life in Dexter. The town benefited greatly from his efforts: he worked to convince the Dexter Shoe Company to locate here; in 1956 he helped bring Camp Dexter to the lake; he was on the school board for many years; and when the local movie house closed, he was instrumental in persuading Dick Reid to keep it open.

Did more of its former students cheer or cry when the old Pleasant Street School was razed in 1969? Several generations of Dexter residents had their first experience with the outside world here. The school was built around 1886, on a site originally given to the town by Jonathan Farrar as common land. Now the town's ice skating rink, it still echoes with children's gleeful voices.

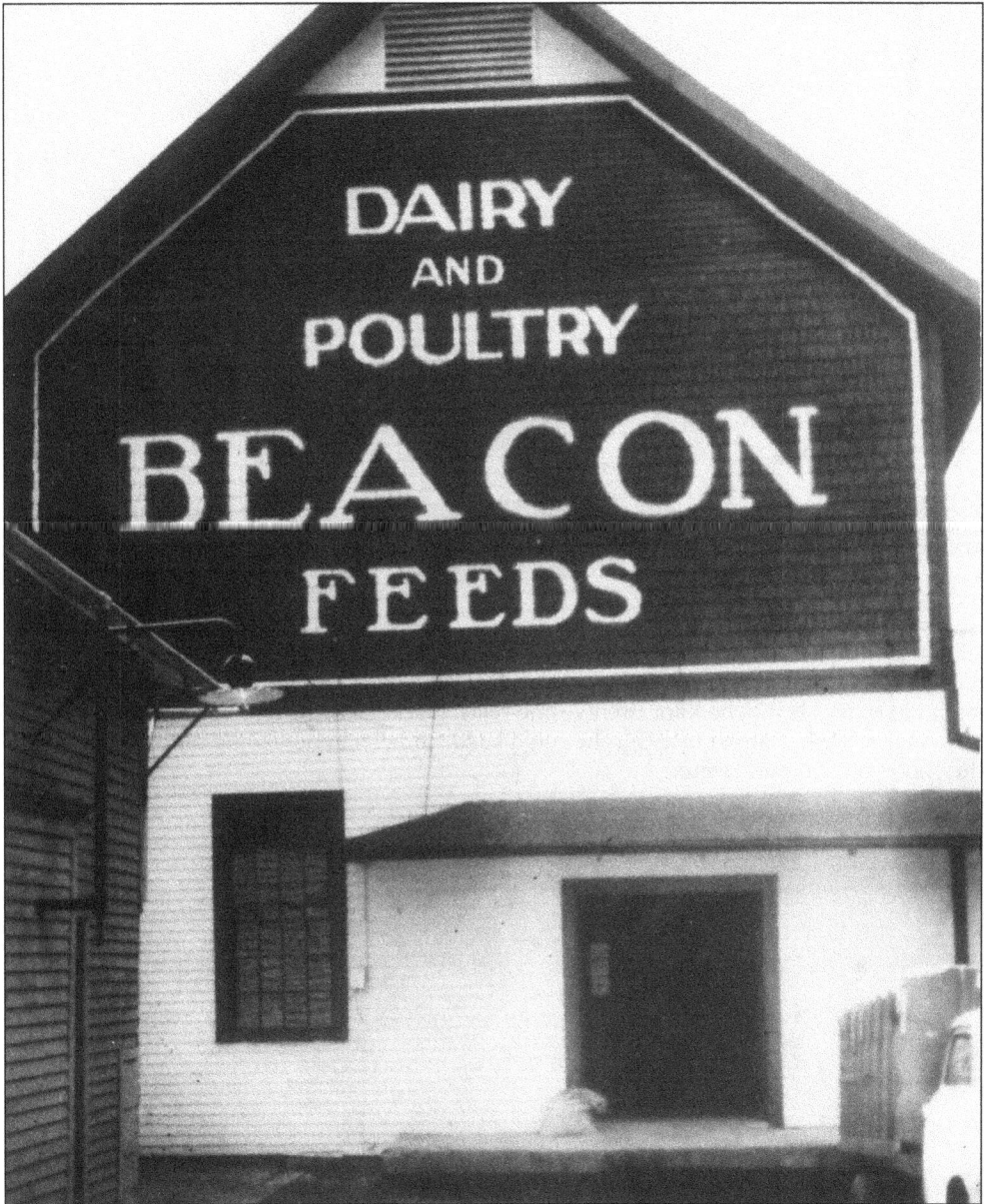

S.L. Small's Grist Mill as it appeared during the late 1950s. The mill was built in 1854 on the site of a previous mill built in 1818, and had numerous additions over the years. Stones were used to grind the grain until the early 1900s, when machine grinding replaced the stones. The mill operated until 1965, and remained water-powered until the end. At the time of its closing it was being run by Clair and Helen Wilkins. The town purchased the mill and the adjoining miller's house and scheduled the buildings for destruction. A number of citizens petitioned the selectmen to allow the museum to be housed in the old mill, and in July 1967 the Grist Mill Museum opened. In 1972 the town removed the mill pond and the little powerhouse in front of the museum. Many Dexter residents can remember the thumping of the waterpumps, the rumbling of the mill, and the slapping of the belts. In addition to powering the Grist Mill, the waterwheel also pumped the town's water to the reservoir on Bryant Hill.

"She was willing to help students anytime. She took an extra interest and even tutored in her home," is how one person remembered Eleanor Hammond. Her name was synonymous with math at Dexter High School for twenty-nine years. She began teaching in Dexter in 1945 and stayed until 1974. Married in 1954, she could be found helping her farmer husband Leon with the chores on many an evening.

Timothy P. Wilson arrived on the scene in August 1966, and athletics at Dexter High School have never been the same. Oh, there were some tough times, but Dexter gained valuable experience. His innovative style and charismatic charm raised Dexter High athletics to new heights. His interest was not only in athletes—many non-athletes benefited from his helpfulness. Shown here are, from left to right: Tim, Spook, and Dave Bolduc.

150

When Roland Goulette and Laddie Wintle went out on wrecker calls they never knew what to expect. Going to a deer/auto collision on the Corinna Road in 1950, they tracked the badly-wounded deer into the woods and finished it off, but not without much difficulty. Game warden Reg Mossey did not appreciate their efforts and promptly confiscated the meat.

This was a familiar sight for many years at the annual Fourth of July parade in Dexter. Roland and Poopie-Do could always be seen weaving in and out of traffic as the parade was enroute to Crosby Park.

"Dexter's worst week for the fire department," is how Ernie Robinson describes it. It was a cold January in 1975 and the week started on Sunday night with a fire in a storage barn behind Otto's potato house. The flames leapt across Church Street in a howling wind and kept the fire crew busy all night. Monday brought a January thaw and a storm dumped heavy rains. The fire department pumped out cellars all that day and night. On Tuesday at 7:00 pm the Titcomb Block caught fire. The fire department spent until 7:00 am Wednesday putting that fire out but were immediately called back later in the morning when Fossa's Block started to burn. They didn't rest again until Thursday. At one time it was feared the entire block was going to burn, similar to the 1907 fire. This photograph of the Titcomb Block was taken Tuesday night, at the peak of the fire's intensity.

Erma Bentley is shown here in period dress at the Grist Mill Museum during the 1976 Bicentennial celebration. Erma was a great storyteller and many anecdotes of Dexter's early citizens have been passed on through her stories. She played the piano at the silent movies in town and sang vocals at the theatre. She also coached the high school plays, and was active in the Favor-Haines Comedy Company.

Vern Bodwell is the local A-T man—that's in Ford model antique autos. His vehicles are a potpourri of parts from every farm rock wall within 25 miles of Dexter, thanks to his many friends and former students pickings. He was Dexter High School's shop teacher for many years. Vern once tried incubating chicken eggs in the shop in a cage attached to the wall; the project ended when the odor drifted through the wall into the adjoining home economics room.

This photograph shows fire chiefs from the recent and distant past: Bert L. Call (left) was fire chief in 1909, and Slim Prescott was chief during the 1960–70 era. Bert was responsible for a major upgrade in the system when he had machinery installed to locate fires quickly. Before that, when there was a fire at the woolen mills, a bell rang and everyone ran to the mills, looked around for smoke, and proceeded from there.

"Here comes the Judge." A gang of them that is, all trying to get in the act at the 1976 Bicentennial horse trot at the old Trotting Park. Avis Shaw got into an accident, but beyond that, all went smoothly. From left to right are: Cliff Goulette, Urban "Ducko" Mountain, Harvey Hatch, Don Susi, and Al Tempesta Sr.

154

"Red" Keyte could be found regularly at the float bridge in his later years. But it wasn't always that way: Red and his brother Harold were two of Dexter's best basketball players in the 1920s. Red was a fireman for many years, and there is a oft-repeated story about the time the fire department took off to fight a fire, but had to return to the firehouse because Red forgot to put his fire pants on.

Mac Hatch at his favorite place in the winter. At this ice house, in 1965, 107 togue were caught—with 38 weighing over 5 pounds. Mac is holding a 6-pounder. Behind Mac are, from left to right: Ricky Fanjoy, Alan Haley, and Ted Clark. Danny Briggs is not far away.

155

"Yankee Independence and limitless curiosity shaped this varied career," the headline said, on December 8, 1977, when the *Eastern Gazette* ran a story on Kenneth Merchant. From clamming as a child in Millbridge to buying a sawmill when he was seventy years old, Ken was on the go all his life. He played basketball and coached in Newport as a young man. He then came to Dexter and was the first auto body repair man here in 1929. In 1942 he started working at Fay and Scott; an expert welder, he welded stainless steel radar and sub-signal boxes in a guarded room during the war for Raytheon. They wanted him to come to Boston to work but he refused. He got some *Applied Hydraulics* magazines from Hovey Harmon and with the information built a hydraulic system and loader for his tractor. "I like to exercise my own mind the way I like to," he would tell the author. At one time he also milked cows and accumulated over 400 acres of fields and woodland. Ken had a plane and used to go fishing in the winter. Orman Gerry, while fishing Nickataous one day, spotted Ken at an obscure lake and flew in. Ken couldn't get his plane started and had a fire going to keep from freezing. "It was no place for a plane to be," said Orman, and he was barely able to get his own plane out. When Orman got home he told his brother; George went in the next day and got plane going by swapping spark plugs back and forth with his warm ones until Ken's plane started.

Kenneth G. Merchant was a worker all his life, but he was slowed down when he had cancer and the prognosis was terminal. "I had no intention of dying," he said while wondering why everyone was suddenly so nice to him. He never recovered from his son's untimely death and had a drinking problem at times later in life. Being with Ken, if you listened hard, you could pick up a few kernels of inspirational wisdom from him as he went about his daily chores.

"The callous palms of the laborers are conversant with finer tissues of self-respect and heroism, whose touch thrills the heart, than the languid fingers of idleness."

Henry David Thoreau

Ken Merchant had a Tailor craft plane in the 1940s and '50s. Ken took chances in his life, and if it wasn't for Orman Gerry one cold winter day, Ken may never have made it (see p. 156).

Kenny and Dana. These two familiar faces have been fixtures in Dexter for a long time now. Every evening Dana checks for unlocked doors and calls the police when he finds one. He has been a part of the fire department and provides vital information when there is a fire. Kenny is everywhere on his bike. He can be seen daily at Tenny's Exxon station helping sweep up or fill gas tanks for the special customers.

Can anyone remember when Bobby Downing wasn't pedaling down the street? Who hasn't bought Christmas cards from him? Even at seventy-five years old, with defective eyesight and the loss of his sense of touch, he still mows lawns and shovels walks. A Dexter resident remembers Bobby's work ethic quite well: "While visiting with a friend . . . I glanced out the window and saw Bobby pushing a wheelbarrow . . . full of leaves he had raked off someone's lawn. He was pushing the wheelbarrow the two miles to the town dump after raking their lawn, and still had to push the wheelbarrow back two miles to town after emptying it. To say the least, I was very impressed with the sense of dedication he had when he went about his work."

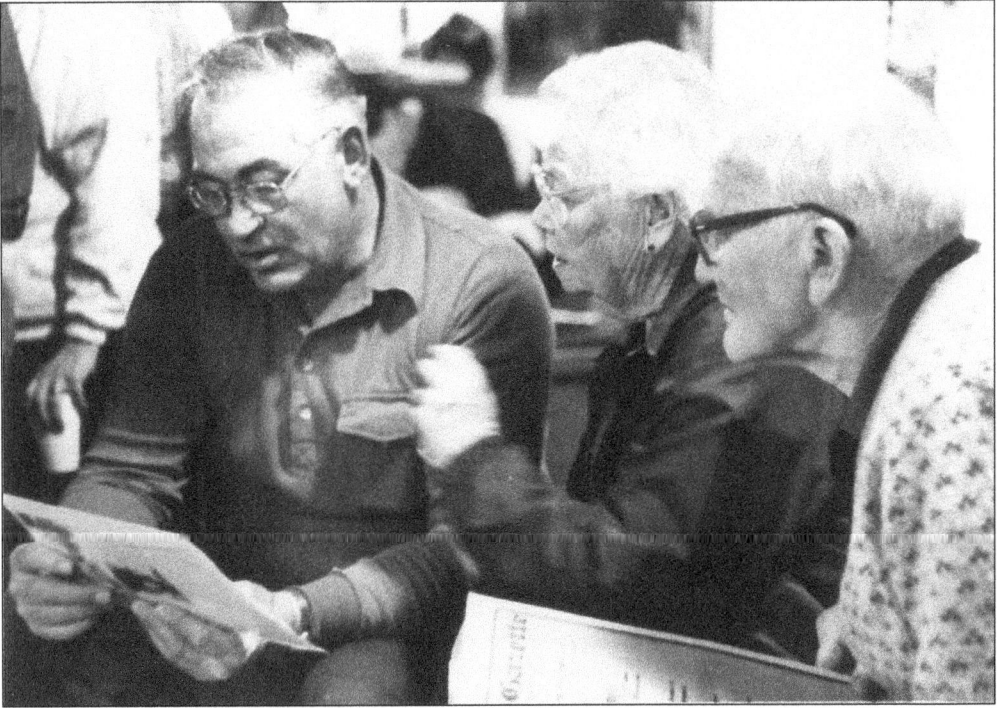

The Ridge Road reunion on April 19, 1995, showed that community spirit is still alive and well in Dexter. Over forty people, most with ties to the Ridge, shared a potluck meal and relived old times in the old Union schoolhouse where many of them went to school. Kay Gray and the Dexter Historical Society teamed up for this nostalgic reunion. Shirley Page (left), Dorothy Brawn (center), and Irl McKusick (right) are shown here looking through old photos.

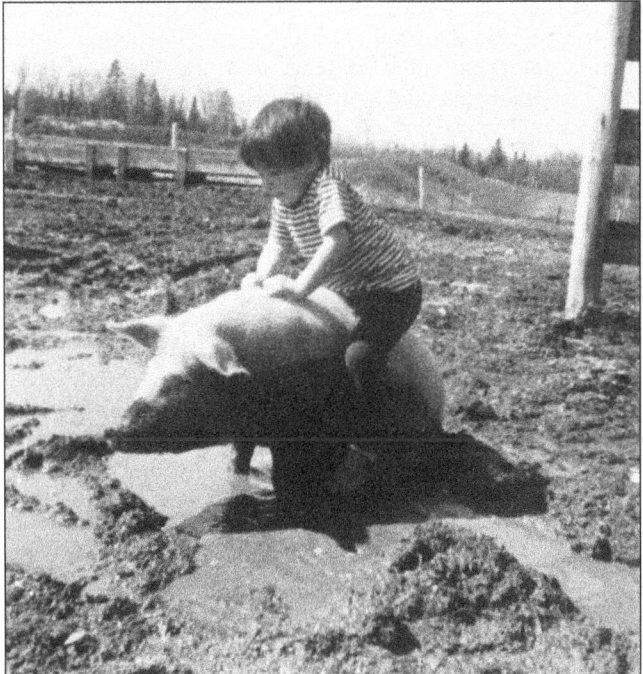

Just as we started this book, with Maria Jennings Keene attempting to drive a pig into the nineteenth century, so we end: with Frankie riding a pig out of the twentieth and into the twenty-first century. The true "spirit of an age" is defined in its youth.

Acknowledgments

This book was a labor of love involving many people. It could not have been done without the resources available at the Dexter Historical Society put together by Rick Whitney. He dug out the needed information from the archives and typed many captions along with his daughter, Emily Whitney. Fred Wintle, Carol Feurtado, Betty Holsapple, and Charlene Page spent many hours digging out information and writing photograph captions. Hilde Bensheimer provided needed recent photographs of sites around Dexter. Dave Pearson drew sketches. John Simco provided photocopy services along with Ann Sidelinker at the University of Maine Printing Services. Photographs were obtained from the *Eastern Gazette*, the *Portland Telegram*, and the *Bangor Daily News*. Dick Shaw of the BDN editorial staff was helpful. The inspiration for this book came from the Camp Dexter Hedge Club, a small close group that meets regularly every summer on the old Camp Dexter grounds and discusses whatever comes to mind. Thank you Eric and Tracy Holsapple, Ed and Sandy Graham, Kevin and Bobbi Holsapple, and Bruce Holsapple for keeping the pressure up and reviewing the techniques used to communicate my thoughts. And finally, thanks to my special friend Donne Lynn Russell, for her proofreading, editing, and the moral support needed to complete this book. Quotes used came from Gordon Chibroski and Shoshana Hoose of the *Portland Sunday Telegram*, Dr. David Smith at the University of Maine, Susan Trausch of the *Boston Globe*, Alice G. Marquis, Ralph Waldo Emerson, and Henry David Thoreau.

www.ingramcontent.com/pod-product-compliance
Lightning Source LLC
Chambersburg PA
CBHW080913100426

42812CB00007B/2262